First World War
and Army of Occupation
War Diary
France, Belgium and Germany

29 DIVISION
Headquarters, Branches and Services
Royal Army Ordnance Corps
Deputy Assistant Director Ordnance Services
28 July 1915 - 31 October 1919

WO95/2290/2

The Naval & Military Press Ltd
www.nmarchive.com
Published in association with The National Archives

Published by

The Naval & Military Press Ltd

Unit 10 Ridgewood Industrial Park,

Uckfield, East Sussex,

TN22 5QE England

Tel: +44 (0) 1825 749494

www.naval-military-press.com

www.nmarchive.com

This diary has been reprinted in facsimile from the original. Any imperfections are inevitably reproduced and the quality may fall short of modern type and cartographic standards.

Contents

Document type	Place/Title	Date From	Date To
Heading	WO95/2290/2 Deputy Assistant Director Ordnance Services 1916 June-1919 Oct		
Heading	29th Division Divl Troops D.A.D.O.S. Jun 1916-Oct 1919		
War Diary	Acheux	03/06/1916	30/06/1916
Heading	War Diary of DADOS 29th Division From 1st July To 31st July 1916 Volume 2		
War Diary	Acheux	01/07/1916	25/07/1916
War Diary	Beauval	27/07/1916	27/07/1916
War Diary	Poperinghe	28/07/1915	28/07/1915
War Diary	Couthove	29/07/1916	31/07/1916
Heading	War Diary of DADOS, 29th Division From 1/8/16 To 31/8/16 Volume III		
War Diary	Poperinghe	01/08/1916	31/08/1916
Heading	War Diary of DADOS, 29th Divl From 1/9/16 To 30/9/16 (Vol IV)		
War Diary	Poperinghe	02/09/1916	28/09/1916
Heading	War Diary of Capt J.H. Grieve, Aud DADOS 29th Div From 1st To 31st Oct 1916 Vol V		
War Diary	Poperinghe	01/10/1916	07/10/1916
War Diary	Corbie	08/10/1916	09/10/1916
War Diary	Ribemont	10/10/1916	19/10/1916
War Diary	E 11 Central	20/10/1916	29/10/1916
War Diary	E.10.a	30/10/1916	31/10/1916
Heading	War Diary of Capt. J.H Grieve, AUD DADOS 29th Division From 1/11/16 To 30/11/16 Vol VI		
War Diary	Corbie	01/11/1916	01/11/1916
War Diary	Treux	15/11/1916	15/11/1916
War Diary	Carnoy	18/11/1916	30/11/1916
Heading	War Diary of D.A.D.O.S., 29th Division From March 1st To March 31st, 1917 Volume 1		
War Diary	Maricourt	02/03/1917	04/03/1917
War Diary	Heilly	05/03/1917	20/03/1917
War Diary	Oissy	21/03/1917	27/03/1917
War Diary	Vignacourt	30/03/1917	31/03/1917
Heading	War Diary of D.A.D.O.S.-29th Division. For The Month Of April, 1917 Volume II		
War Diary	Beauval Lucheux	01/04/1917	04/04/1917
War Diary	Bavincourt	05/04/1917	09/04/1917
War Diary	Wagonlieu	12/04/1917	12/04/1917
War Diary	Arras	13/04/1917	23/04/1917
War Diary	Warlus Couin	25/04/1917	30/04/1917
Heading	War Diary of DADOS 29 Divisional From 1st May 1917 To 31st May 1917 (Volume 1)		
War Diary	Couin	01/05/1917	02/05/1917
War Diary	Arras	03/05/1917	07/05/1917
War Diary	Warlus	08/05/1917	14/05/1917
War Diary	Arras	15/05/1917	31/05/1917
Heading	War Diary For Month of June 1917 From D.A.D.O.S. 29th Division Volume 1		

War Diary	Arras	01/06/1917	01/06/1917
War Diary	Bernaville	03/06/1917	21/06/1917
War Diary	Proven	26/06/1917	26/06/1917
War Diary	Dragon Camp	29/06/1917	19/07/1917
War Diary	Proven	21/07/1917	31/07/1917
War Diary	Proven	21/07/1917	06/08/1917
War Diary	J Camp	08/08/1917	28/08/1917
War Diary	Proven	29/08/1917	31/08/1917
Heading	War Diary From 1st September 1917 To 30th September 1917 D.A.D.O.S. 29th Division Volume XXXI		
War Diary	Proven	02/09/1917	21/09/1917
War Diary	J Camp	22/09/1917	05/10/1917
War Diary	International Corner	06/10/1917	10/10/1917
War Diary	Watou Rd.	11/10/1917	14/10/1917
War Diary	Basseux	17/10/1917	30/10/1917
Heading	War Diary of D.A.D.O.S., 29th Divn 1-11-17 To 30-11-17 Vol. XXXIII		
War Diary	Basseux	01/11/1917	15/11/1917
War Diary	Moislains	17/11/1917	18/11/1917
War Diary	Sorel	19/11/1917	30/11/1917
Heading	No. 29 Div. Supply Column War Diary For The Month Of December 1917. Volume No. 21		
War Diary	Sorel	01/12/1917	03/12/1917
War Diary	Le Cauroy	05/12/1917	14/12/1917
War Diary	Hucqueliers	18/12/1917	19/12/1917
War Diary	Hesdin	20/12/1917	31/12/1917
War Diary	In The Field	01/12/1917	30/12/1917
War Diary	Hesdin Wizernes	02/01/1918	18/01/1918
War Diary	Merey Camp Vlamertinghe	19/01/1918	25/01/1918
War Diary	Road Camp Vlamertinghe	27/01/1918	09/02/1918
War Diary	Steenvoorde	11/02/1918	28/02/1918
Heading	War Diary D A D O S 29 Div 1-31 March 1918 Vol. 37		
War Diary	Steenvoorde	02/03/1918	04/03/1918
War Diary	Road Camp Vlamertinghe	06/03/1918	17/03/1918
War Diary	Dirty Bucket Camp Vlamertinghe	20/03/1918	09/04/1918
War Diary	Leparc	10/04/1918	10/04/1918
War Diary	Morbecque	11/04/1918	11/04/1918
War Diary	Caestre	12/04/1918	12/04/1918
War Diary	St Sylvestre	14/04/1918	18/04/1918
War Diary	Hondeghem	19/04/1918	26/04/1918
War Diary	Wallon Cappel	28/04/1918	21/06/1918
War Diary	Wardrecques	22/06/1918	21/07/1918
War Diary	Bavinchove	22/07/1918	01/08/1918
War Diary	Near Les Cinq Rucs	03/08/1918	01/09/1918
War Diary	Hazebrouck	02/09/1918	05/09/1918
War Diary	Fletre	07/09/1918	07/09/1918
War Diary	Hazebrouck	11/09/1918	17/09/1918
War Diary	Watou	18/09/1918	27/09/1918
War Diary	Brake Camp	28/09/1918	06/10/1918
War Diary	Vlamertinghe	07/10/1918	12/10/1918
War Diary	Ypres	13/10/1918	13/10/1918
War Diary	Molenhoek	15/10/1918	15/10/1918
War Diary	Ledeghem	16/10/1918	19/10/1918
War Diary	Nr Courtrai	21/10/1918	25/10/1918

War Diary	Mouveaux	27/10/1918	06/11/1918
War Diary	Rolleghem	07/11/1918	08/11/1918
War Diary	St Genois	10/11/1918	12/11/1918
War Diary	Renaix	14/11/1918	14/11/1918
War Diary	Flobecq	15/11/1918	15/11/1918
War Diary	Enghien	18/11/1918	18/11/1918
War Diary	Tubize	21/11/1918	22/11/1918
War Diary	Braine L'Alleud	23/11/1918	23/11/1918
War Diary	Ottignies	24/11/1918	24/11/1918
War Diary	Nil Abbesse	25/11/1918	25/11/1918
War Diary	Grand-Rosiere	27/11/1918	27/11/1918
War Diary	Huy	28/11/1918	28/11/1918
War Diary	Anthisnes	30/11/1918	30/11/1918
War Diary	Sprimont	01/12/1918	01/12/1918
War Diary	Niveze	02/12/1918	02/12/1918
War Diary	Malmedy	04/12/1918	04/12/1918
War Diary	Kalterherberg	05/12/1918	05/12/1918
War Diary	Kesternich	06/12/1918	06/12/1918
War Diary	Zulpich	07/12/1918	07/12/1918
War Diary	Efferen	08/12/1918	13/12/1918
War Diary	Bensberg	14/12/1918	17/12/1918
War Diary	Sand	21/12/1918	21/12/1918
War Diary	Odenthal	22/12/1918	29/12/1918
Heading	Rhine Army Southern Division Late 29th Division Dep. Asst Dir. Ordnance Services Jan-Oct 1919		
War Diary	Odenthal	01/01/1919	27/05/1919
War Diary	Odenthal Germany	28/05/1919	10/06/1919
War Diary	Odenthal	11/06/1919	31/07/1919
War Diary	Odenthal Germany	01/08/1919	29/09/1919
War Diary	Odenthal	30/09/1919	31/10/1919

WO95/2290

1/2 Deputy Assistant Director Ordnance Services

1916 June - 1919 Oct.

29TH DIVISION

DIVL TROOPS

D. A. D. O. S.

JUN 1916 - OCT 1919

Army Form C. 2118.

Instructions regarding War Diaries and Intelligence Summaries are contained in F. S. Regs., Part II. and the Staff Manual respectively. Title Pages will be prepared in manuscript.

WAR DIARY
or
~~INTELLIGENCE~~ SUMMARY
(Erase heading not required.)

DADOS 29 Div
Vol 1

Place	Date	Hour	Summary of Events and Information	Remarks and references to Appendices
ACHEUX	3/6/16	2300	Raid by 1/Lancs. Fus. into enemy trenches. No enemy found; no casualties. JHG	
"	6/6/16		Moved store from Sucrerie to barn in ACHEUX, as former being intermittently shelled. JHG	
"	10/6/16	1600	ADOS. came to ACHEUX and inspected office and store. JHG	
"	14/6/16	2300	"Daylight saving" started by putting clock forward 1 hour JHG	
"	15/6/16	1000	Conference at ADOS. office. Chief subject of discussion – salving of important stores in the event of an advance. JHG	
"	22/6/16	1000	Conference at ADOS office. Chief subject of discussion – method of distributing stores to units in event of an advance. JHG	
"	24/6/16	0600	Bombardment of enemy lines started, preparatory to attack JHG	
"	25/6/16		Bombardment continued. JHG	
"	26/6/16		" . Raid by 1/Border Regt.; wire not cut.	
"	27/6/16		" . Raid by 1/Newfoundland Regt. Enemy found in force JHG	
"	28/6/16		Attack postponed on account of weather. Heavy rain JHG	
"	29/6/16		Bombardment continued. Raid by 1/Essex. JHG	
"	30/6/16		" Weather improved. JHG	

June 16 to Dec 18

2449 Wt. W14957/M90 750,000 1/16 J.B.C. & A. Forms/C.2118/12.

Vol 52

CONFIDENTIAL

War Diary

of

DADOS 29th Division

from 1st July to 31st July
1916

Volume 1

Instructions regarding War Diaries and Intelligence Summaries are contained in F. S. Regs., Part II. and the Staff Manual respectively. Title Pages will be prepared in manuscript.

WAR DIARY
or
~~INTELLIGENCE SUMMARY~~
(Erase heading not required.)

Army Form C. 2118.

Place	Date	Hour	Summary of Events and Information	Remarks and references to Appendices
ACHEUX	1/7/16	730	General attack started. Heavy casualties and ultimately no ground gained. Instructions given that no steel helmets be evacuated with casualties.	
"	2/7/16	1100	ADOS called to collect details of gun parts demanded during week's bombardment to ~~obtain~~ make estimate of parts most required during similar future bombardments. About 200 steel helmets collected from C.C.S. and brought to store.	
"	3/7/16		Arrangements made with R.O.O. for dealing with casualty equipment the first of which despatched at night under arrangements made by DAQMG.	
"	4/7/16		Visited all Q.M.s, explaining details of salvage for surplus stores.	
"	6/7/16		Conference at ADOS office, MARIEUX. Informed that VIII Corps joins Reserve Army.	
"	7/7/16		To AMIENS for buckets to drain trenches after heavy rain. About 700 steel helmets salved from Railhead. Re-equipping of Division proceeding largely with stores collected from dumps by W.O.s, and redistributed instead of being evacuated. W.O.s supervising work of salvage dumps and keeping in constant touch with units' requirements, thus minimizing necessity of demanding stores in replacement from Base. Four Stokes mortars, to replace losses received.	
"	8/7/16		Lists of losses in action compiled in order to re-equip as soon as possible. Stores collected from Railhead to meet same requirements as	
"	10/7/16		Fourteen out of the 39 Lewis guns, which were taken forward in the attack, recovered, by night patrols.	
"	11/7/16		The fourteen guns despatched to Base.	
"	12/7/16		Two 3" Stokes mortars, lost in advanced posts, recovered	

Army Form C. 2118.

WAR DIARY
or
INTELLIGENCE SUMMARY
(Erase heading not required.)

Instructions regarding War Diaries and Intelligence Summaries are contained in F. S. Regs., Part II. and the Staff Manual respectively. Title Pages will be prepared in manuscript.

Place	Date	Hour	Summary of Events and Information	Remarks and references to Appendices
ACHEUX	13/7/16		In connection with plan, in future attacks, to wear anti-gas helmets pinned to front of jackets, for rapid adjustment over head, went to Amiens to buy safety pins. JHG	
"	14/7/16		Visited Railhead, to go through stores available with R.O.O., to meet deficiencies and prevent stores required by this Div.n, returned by another Div.n, being despatched to Base. JHG	
"	15/7/16		To D.S.C. workshop at BEAUVAL, to ask them to make some pattern of muzzle cup holder, and fix rod to base plugs of Mills bombs, for firing same from rifles. JHG	
"	17/7/16		To Doullens to buy safety pins for fixing gas helmets to jackets JHG	
"	18/7/16		Make experiments with firing Mills grenades from rifle; rod attachment having been made to grenade. Different lengths of rod tried to get right length of flight. JHG	
"	19/7/16		To Amiens to give orders for battle stores, in view of future operations. Steel helmets again arriving. JHG	
"	20/7/16		Conference at Marieux with D.D.S.T. [?] Suggested that salved stores should be kept at Railhead for a few days, instead of being immediately evacuated, so that Div.ns could pick out stores urgently required. JHG	
"	22/7/16		Brought back battle stores from Amiens. Informed in evening that Div.n being moved, and wired to Base to suspend issues pending move. JHG	
"	23/7/16		Surplus stores loaded onto rail for despatch to new railhead. Trench stores and special Corps stores stacked separately for handing over to incoming Div.n	
"	24/7/16		Went round Batt.n dumps and cleared out some stores that units could not carry. Increase of transport has apparently not kept pace with increase of equipment. Sent all equipment thus collected to railhead for despatch to new area. JHG	

2449 Wt. W14957/M90 750,000 1/16 J.B.C. & A. Forms/C.2118/12.

Army Form C. 2118.

Instructions regarding War Diaries and Intelligence Summaries are contained in F. S. Regs., Part II. and the Staff Manual respectively. Title Pages will be prepared in manuscript.

WAR DIARY
or
INTELLIGENCE SUMMARY
(Erase heading not required.)

Place	Date	Hour	Summary of Events and Information	Remarks and references to Appendices
ACHEUX	25/7/16		Handed over trench stores etc to DADOS 25th DIV. Left by motor to ~~BEAUVAL~~, where Div. H.Q. stopping.	
BEAUVAL	27/7/16		Left BEAUVAL at midday by motor to POPERINGHE via ST POL & HAZEBROUCK. Visited 6th Div. H.Q., and saw DADOS 6th Div. and discussed handing over of his stores etc.	
POPERINGHE	28/7/16		Moved out with Div. H.Q. to COUTHODE. Went to ARNEKE, railhead, to arrange to have stores arriving there re-consigned to POPERINGHE, as distance from ARNEKE to H.Q. would make it impossible to clear trucks as they arrived daily.	
COUTHOVE	29/7/16		Notified that trucks being re-consigned. Went to POPERINGHE Station to inform R.O.O., so that trucks might be placed in yard at some point where lorries could conveniently unload.	
"	30/7/16		Sent all lorries and store party to station at 7 AM to start clearing 5 trucks arrived.	
"	31/7/16		Reserve of gas helmets from ACHEUX re-consigned here; [illegible] with 6th Div. taken over in exchange.	

[illegible] Capt.
DADOS 6th Div.

Vol 3

CONFIDENTIAL

WAR DIARY

OF

DADOS, 29th DIVISION

FROM 1/8/16 to 31/8/16.

VOLUME III.

Army Form C. 2118.

Instructions regarding War Diaries and Intelligence Summaries are contained in F. S. Regs., Part II. and the Staff Manual respectively. Title Pages will be prepared in manuscript.

WAR DIARY
or
~~INTELLIGENCE SUMMARY~~
(Erase heading not required.)

Place	Date	Hour	Summary of Events and Information	Remarks and references to Appendices
POPERINGHE	1/8/16		Moved from COUTHOVE to POPERINGHE. Took over Ordnance Office and Stores from O.O. 6th Div. JHG	
"	2/8/16		Trucks of stores consigned from ACHEUX arrived; issuing of stores started. JHG	
"	5/8/16		A.D.O.S. inspected office and stores. JHG	
"	7/8/16		Received, and started to issue, P.H.G. helmets to all ranks, to replace one P.H. helmets. All ranks now carry one P.H. & one P.H.G. helmet. JHG	
"	8/8/16		Heavy gas attack. P.H. helmets used replaced at once by new P.H.G. JHG	
"	9/8/16		All Brigades instructed to send in 2 armourers, to make number in armourers shop 6. Work in shop largely consists in repairing bicycles, which has become a heavy item. JHG	
"	10/8/16		Lt Col Man left Corps, and Lt Col Stewart took over duties of A.D.O.S.	
"	11/8/16		Col. Hale, DDOS Second Army, inspected stores and office.	
"	16/8/16		A.D.O.S. made thorough inspection of office arrangements. JHG	
"	17/8/16		Conference at A.D.O.S. To save 1st Line transport, Ordnance lorries started to deliver stores to Inf. Brigades. Stores drawn and laid out in morning, and delivered in afternoon. System satisfactory. JHG	
"	19/8/16		Drew deflection dials from Second Army workshop for 2" Mortars.	
"	24/8/16		Artillery re-organized into 6-gun batteries, thus eliminating 1 Brigade, to economize personnel. JHG	
"	31/8/16		Instructions received to demand blankets to complete to 1 per man, since 1st Line scale had been 25% of strength only. JHG	

Vol 4

CONFIDENTIAL

WAR DIARY

OF

D.A.D.O.S., 29th Divn

FROM 1/9/16 to 30/9/16.

(VOL. IV).

Instructions regarding War Diaries and Intelligence Summaries are contained in F. S. Regs., Part II. and the Staff Manual respectively. Title Pages will be prepared in manuscript.

WAR DIARY
or
~~INTELLIGENCE SUMMARY~~
(Erase heading not required.)

Army Form C. 2118.

Place	Date	Hour	Summary of Events and Information	Remarks and references to Appendices
POPERINGHE	2/9/16		Steel helmets to complete all units to 1 per man received. [illegible]	
"	3/9/16		New pattern small box respirators started to arrive. [illegible]	
"	7/9/16		First consignment of gum boots thigh for winter issue received [illegible]	
"	10/9/16		Lewis gun hand carts issued to half scale. [illegible]	
"	18/9/16		Second half issue of Lewis hand carts received, for all units except Pioneer Battalion.	
"	22/9/16		Large consignment of periscopes received, to meet outstanding deficiencies [illegible]	
"	28/9/16		Experimental carriers, for M.G belt boxes, with attachments for fixing to equipment in the place of a pack, made in armourers shop and issued to 88th M.G. Co. Carriers made to contain 2 belt boxes. Fourteen of them made and issued. By carrying the ammunition in this way, the man's hands are left free for using his rifle etc. [illegible]	

Vol 5

CONFIDENTIAL

WAR DIARY OF

CAPT. J. H. GRIEVE, A.O.D.
DADOS, 29th Divn
from 1st to 31st Octr 1916

VOL V

Instructions regarding War Diaries and Intelligence Summaries are contained in F. S. Regs., Part II. and the Staff Manual respectively. Title Pages will be prepared in manuscript.

WAR DIARY
or
~~INTELLIGENCE SUMMARY~~

(Erase heading not required.)

Army Form C. 2118.

Place	Date	Hour	Summary of Events and Information	Remarks and references to Appendices
POPERINGHE	1/10/16		26 Lewis guns received, to complete Batty to 10 guns each.	
"	2/10/16		Instructions to prepare to leave VIII Corps received. DADOS 55th Div. arrived to take over.	
"	6/10/16		Despatched all surplus stores in 12 lorries to PROVEN, for railing to new destination. Handed over office and stores to DADOS 55th Div.	
"	7/10/16		Left POPERINGHE by train at 7 P.M.	
CORBIE	8/10/16		Detrained at SALEUX at 11 A.M.; thence by road to CORBIE, which office opened temporarily. Attached to XIV Corps.	
"	9/10/16		In AMIENS arranging for saddle bags, to carry rations etc up to front line beyond FLERS, where wheeled traffic was impossible owing to lack of roads in area over which advance had been made.	
RIBEMONT	10/10/16		Div. transferred to XV Corps. Moved from Corbie to RIBEMONT; saw ADOS XV Corps en route at HEILLY.	
"	11/10/16		Collected helmets from Salvage dumps for reinforcements. A fair number available: but more help in re-equipping could be given by Salvage dumps if they were converted into advanced Depots with an O.O. in charge, who could decide what to keep, what to destroy, and what to despatch to Base.	
"	12/10/16		More helmets collected. In afternoon attack by 1/Essex and 1/Newfoundland. 120 prisoners and 3 machine guns captured by latter.	
"	13/10/16		Visited advanced Bde H.Q. of 88 Bde, to find out urgent requirements after their action of previous day.	
"	15/10/16		Took over 4000 gum boots from 41st Div. at their dump near ALBERT.	

Army Form C. 2118.

WAR DIARY
or
~~INTELLIGENCE SUMMARY~~ II

(Erase heading not required.)

Instructions regarding War Diaries and Intelligence Summaries are contained in F. S. Regs., Part II. and the Staff Manual respectively. Title Pages will be prepared in manuscript.

Place	Date	Hour	Summary of Events and Information	Remarks and references to Appendices
RIBEMONT	16/10/16		Despatched to Base 11,500 P.H. helmets, reducing Div. reserve of P.H. helmets to 2,500 as Divn equipped throughout with small box respirators.	
"	17/10/16		Second attack by 88th Bde (2/Hants and 4/Worcesters). 170 prisoners taken SHS	
"	19/10/16		Moved from RIBEMONT to E11 central, near ALBERT, Div. rear H.Q. into hutments SHS	
E 11 Central	20/10/16		Pitched store tents and arranged new dump at E10a. Took over 12th D.A.; 12th Div. going back into rest.	
"	21/10/16		First consignments of special winter clothing received, and distribution started SHS	
"	22/10		Leather jerkins received. SHS	
"	24/10/16		To advanced D.H.Q. to see Q.M.s of 87th Bde. Chief complaint about boots repaired by Calais not being watertight. SHS	
"	25/10/16		To HEILLY to see ADOS about getting supply of extra winter underclothing, owing to impossibility of washing or drying clothing in possession of troops. Through bad weather men always more or less soaked. Arranged to store surplus, when received, at XV Corps baths. SHS	
"	28/10/16		Move warning sent round. SHS	
"	29/10/16		Instructed to hand over dump site and store of gum boots to 1st Australian Div.; but they decided not to take over. Various orders published as regards move, on 1st Australian taking over the line from 29th	
E.10.a	30/10/16		Div. transferred to XIV Corps. H.Q. moved to CORBIE. Stopped at E10a in camp, for convenience of being near railhead (ALBERT).	
"	31/10/16		Moved from E11a to CORBIE with office, to join D.H.Q., on transfer of Railhead SHS	

2449 Wt. W14957/M90 750,000 1/16 J.B.C. & A. Forms/C.2118/12.

Vol 6

CONFIDENTIAL

WAR DIARY
OF

CAPT. J. H GRIEVE, A.O.D.

DADOS 29th DIVISION

FROM 1/11/16 to 30/11/16.

VOL. VI.

Army Form C. 2118.

Instructions regarding War Diaries and Intelligence Summaries are contained in F. S. Regs., Part II. and the Staff Manual respectively. Title Pages will be prepared in manuscript.

WAR DIARY
or
~~INTELLIGENCE SUMMARY~~

(Erase heading not required.)

Place	Date	Hour	Summary of Events and Information	Remarks and references to Appendices
CORBIE	1/11/16		Last lorry loads of stores moved from E10a to CORBIE, and Trucks arriving at latter place for refitting of Div. while resting. Monthly review of outstanding indents started. etc	
TREUX	15/11/16		Moved from CORBIE to TREUX, on way back to forward area. Railhead at PLATEAU. Lorries not allowed in forward area; therefore all drawing of stores carried out by G.S. wagons etc.	
CARNOY	18/11/16		Moved from TREUX to CARNOY camp.	
	30/11/16		All 2nd blankets received; most of them stored at CORBIE, to be available for issue to troops when moved into Reserve. etc	

J H Brien Capt
DADOS
3/12/16.

2449 Wt. W14957/M90 750,000 1/16 J.B.C. & A. Forms/C.2118/12.

C O N F I D E N T I A L.

W A R   D I A R Y

of

D.A.D.O.S., 29th D I V I S I O N.

From MARCH ~~2nd~~ 1st to MARCH 31st, 1917.

VOLUME 1.

Vol 10

29

Instructions regarding War Diaries and Intelligence Summaries are contained in F. S. Regs., Part II. and the Staff Manual respectively. Title Pages will be prepared in manuscript.

WAR DIARY

~~or~~

~~INTELLIGENCE~~ SUMMARY

(Erase heading not required.)

March 1917

Army Form C. 2118.

Place	Date	Hour	Summary of Events and Information	Remarks and references to Appendices
Maricourt	2 March		Area Stores sent to O.O. XIV Corps Troops	
"	4	"	Orders to move recd	
Heilly	5	"	Ordnance moved to Heilly	
"	7	"	Division training in Reserve area	
"	11	"	Lewis gun butts strengthened by wire binding	
"	13	"	Lewis guns overhauled	
"	14	"	Capt. Greive went on leave. Capt. Gee took over duties of DADOS	
"	15	"	Special Order of the Day issued embodying awards for other ranks	
"	17	"	British troops occupy Bapaume	
"	18	"	Division ordered to move to Cavillon Area	
"	20	"	Division move to Cavillon completed	
Oissy	21	"	Ordnance moved to Oissy	
"	23	"	Capt. Greive returned & took over duties of DADOS from Capt. Gee	
"	24	"	Summer time came into force at 11 pm. Undercoats for leather jerkins called in. Petrol tins issued for water supply. 29th Artillery returned from Somme & administered by DADOS. Box Respirators & 1" Very Pistols sent in by Infantry Units.	
"	27	"	Orders for a move received	
Vignacourt	30	"	Ordnance moved to Vignacourt	
"	31		All Units resting	

[illegible] Capt AOD

DADOS 29 Div

31 III 17

2449 Wt. W14957/M90 750,000 1/16 J.B.C. & A. Forms/C.2118/12.

C O N F I D E N T I A L.

W A R D I A R Y

of

D.A.D.O.S. - 29th DIVISION.

For the Month of APRIL, 1917

Volume II.

Instructions regarding War Diaries and Intelligence Summaries are contained in F. S. Regs., Part II. and the Staff Manual respectively. Title Pages will be prepared in manuscript.

WAR DIARY

~~or~~

~~INTELLIGENCE SUMMARY~~

(Erase heading not required.)

April 1917

Army Form C. 2118.

Place	Date	~~Hour~~	Summary of Events and Information	Remarks and references to Appendices
Beauval	1	April	Ordnance moved to Beauval	
Lucheux	2	"	" " Lucheux Capt. Greive left the Division Capt. Gee took over duties of DADOS.	
"	4	"	Lucheux Divl Dump formed for surplus kit &c. Some of the 1½" Very Pistols returned by Infantry issued to Artillery	
Bavincourt	5	"	Ordnance moved to Bavincourt	
"	9	"	Third Army offensive commenced	
Wagnonlieu	12	"	Ordnance moved to Wagnonlieu. Div went into the Line. Box Respirators issued to Units on line of ~~march~~	
Arras	13	"	Ordnance moved to Arras.	
"	14	"	Lieut Smith took over duties of DADOS from Capt: Gee	
"	16	"	Stores & Armourers Shop moved to fresh billets	
"	17	"	DADOS Office moved to fresh billet	
"	19	"	Very large Indents being received from Units owing to heavy losses in recent fighting	
"	22	"	Great improvement in weather	
"	23	"	Another attack by the Division	
Warlus	25	"	2nd Anniversary of the Dardanelles Landing. Division came out of the line. Ordnance moved to Warlus	
Couin	26	"	Ordnance moved to Couin. Refitting of Division commenced	
"	27	"	Divl Artillery and attached Units handed over to DADOS 3rd Division to administer	
"	29	"	Heavy demands for Box Respirators for reinforcements	
"	30	"	Conference of Quartermasters. 51 Lewis & 9 Vickers guns received from Third Army Gun Park	

[illegible] Lieut. AOD

30 IV. 17 DADOS. 29 Div.

2449 Wt. W14957/M90 750,000 1/16 J.B.C. & A. Forms/C.2118/12.

Confidential

DADOS 29 Div Vol 12

War Diary

of

D.A.D.O.S 29th Division

From 1st May 1917 to 31st May 1917

(Volume 1.)

Instructions regarding War Diaries and Intelligence Summaries are contained in F. S. Regs., Part II. and the Staff Manual respectively. Title Pages will be prepared in manuscript.

WAR DIARY
~~or~~
~~INTELLIGENCE SUMMARY~~
(Erase heading not required.)

May 1917

Army Form C. 2118.

Place	Date	Hour	Summary of Events and Information	Remarks and references to Appendices
Couin	1	May	Finished refitting Division. Division fully equipped with Machine Guns. Recd visit from ADOS XVIII Corps	
"	2	"	Division moved to Arras. Formed a temporary dump at Saulty.	
Arras	3	"	DADOS Stores moved to Arras. All battle Stores due in hand [illegible]. Saulty dump cleared.	
"	5	"	Went to Doullens to purchase brooms. 1500 Horse Box Respirators recd.	
"	7	"	87 Bde. moved to Duisans, 88 Bde to Berneville.	
Warlus	8	"	Divl HQrs & Ordnance moved to Warlus. Visited all the Brigades. Specialists Armbands urgently required	
"	9	"	Went with DAQMG to Corbielle [illegible] & Pas. Arranged to clear Divl dumps of blankets &c.	
"	11	"	88th Bde moved to Arras & 86th Bde to Berneville. Administration of Artillery 29th Divn taken over from DADOS 3rd Division	
"	12	"	Division ordered to be equipped with Goggles anti gas Sponge in place of ordinary Goggles anti-gas [illegible] Dump cleared	
"	13	"	87th Bde. moved to Arras. Division applied for Strombos Horns & other Trench Stores.	
"	14	"	Went to Avesnes & Doullens. Attended Conference at ADOS VI Corps Divisions.	
Arras	15	"	Divl HQrs & Ordnance moved to Arras.	
"	16	"	Went to Amiens. Office Stores & workshops moved to Place St Croix from Rue Lamartine.	
"	17	"	117 Sets of Packsaddlery received from 3rd Divn	
"	18	"	ADOS VI Corps visited here.	
"	20	"	Visited HQ Divl Artly, HQ 3 Inf. Bdes. & Pioneer Battn. 100 Yukon packs arrived.	
"	23	"	Visited ADOS VI Corps. 155 A. Fd. Bde transferred to Third Army	
"	24	"	Large number of magazines & [illegible] received from Third Army Gun PK	
"	25	"	Serious explosion in yard where Ordnance Storehouses are situated. 11 men wounded (5 Ordnance 6 details attached), 1 man (detail) subsequently died. Court of Enquiry held by Order of Divl HQrs	
"	27	"	Pte Marsden AOC died from injuries recd. on 25th.	
"	31	"	Orders for move received.	

31 V 17.

[illegible] Lieut
DADOS 29 Divn

2449 Wt. W14957/M90 750,000 1/16 J.B.C. & A. Forms/C.2118/12.

Confidential.　　Vol 13

War Diary for month of June 1917

From D.A.D.O.S.

29th Division

Volume. 1.

Army Form C. 2118.

WAR DIARY
~~or~~
~~INTELLIGENCE SUMMARY~~

(Erase heading not required.)

Instructions regarding War Diaries and Intelligence Summaries are contained in F. S. Regs., Part II. and the Staff Manual respectively. Title Pages will be prepared in manuscript.

June 1917

Place	Date	Hour	Summary of Events and Information	Remarks and references to Appendices
Arras	1	June	Recd visit from DADOS 3rd Divn arranged transfer of VI Corps Stores.	
Bernaville	3	"	Ordnance moved from Arras to Bernaville. DHQ moved to Warlus.	
"	4	"	DHQ moved to Bernaville. Railhead Risel	
"	5	"	Move of Division to Bernaville Area completed.	
"	6	"	Visited 87 & 88 Bdes & Quartermasters	
"	7	"	ADOS XIX Corps visited here. Discussed question of obtaining cloth. IOM. 18 & 31 Light Shops visited here went with him round all the Brigades & Transport lines.	
"	9	"	Divl Bombing School established at Mt Renault.	
"	14	"	Examination of Vickers guns completed. Recd visit from IOM 18 & 31 Light Shops.	
"	15	"	Went to Abbeville to purchase 2000 yards of rope.	
"	16	"	Divl Horse Show.	
"	17	"	Visited Brigades. Sample made of new waistcoat carrier for Lewis Magazines. 11 Lewis Guns recd for Middlesex Regt	
"	19	"	Capt. Smith proceeded on leave. Capt. Bell took over duties of DADOS	
	21	"	Visited Brigades	
Proven	26	"	DHQ & Ordnance moved to Proven in Fifth Army XIV Corps.	
Dragon Camp	29	"	DHQ & Ordnance moved to Dragon Camp. 29 Divn relieved 38 Divn in the line	
"	30	"	Railhead International Corner	

A. Smith Capt.
DADOS. 29 Divn
1 July 1917

2449 Wt. W14957/M90 750,000 1/16 J.B.C. & A. Forms/C.2118/12.

Instructions regarding War Diaries and Intelligence Summaries are contained in F. S. Regs., Part II. and the Staff Manual respectively. Title Pages will be prepared in manuscript.

WAR DIARY
~~or~~
~~INTELLIGENCE SUMMARY~~

(Erase heading not required.)

July 1917

Army Form C. 2118.

Place	Date	Hour	Summary of Events and Information	Remarks and references to Appendices
Dragon Camp	1	July	Capt. Evans returned from leave & took over duties of DADOS from Capt. Bell. Recd. visit from C.I.O.M.	
"	2	"	Went to Dunkirk to purchase stores.	
"	4	"	Went to XVIII Corps School Volkeringkhove & arranged about return of Lewis Guns	
"	5	"	Recd. 194 Yukon Packs to make Division up to 250. Visited Divl. Bomb Dump & Divl. Salvage Off.	
"	6	"	Recd. 198 sets of packsaddlery. 30 issued to O.O. XIV Corps Troops.	
"	7	"	Visited 86 & 87 Bdes. I.O.M. XIV Corps. D.D.O.S. & C.I.O.M. Fifth Army.	
"	8	"	Fifth Army Gun Park opened.	
"	9	"	Visited O.O. XIV Troops. 14 Carriages Ambulance recd.	
"	10	"	Pouches Magazine Web 2400 & Cutch 112 lbs received. A.D.O.S. XIV Corps brought 24 Clinometers Field for	M.G. Coys.
"	12	"	Visited Camp at Proven with A.A. & Q.M.G. Went to Dunkirk purchasing. 2000 water bottles & carriers arrived	
"	13	"	Went to Bailleul purchasing. Recd. copper washers for T.M.B.	
"	15	"	Went to Proven re new Ordnance Dump. Recd. visit from A.D.O.S. XIV Corps	
"	16	"	Special Stores received 120 Yukon Packs. 88 - 18 pdrs & 115 - 4.5" Ammn. Carriers. 150 Boxes Belt Ammn for Vickers Guns. 46 Trench Mountings for M.G. barrage fire. 200 anti-gas alarm rattles.	
"	19	"	Went to Dunkirk purchasing. Arranged to issue stores at refilling points	
Proven	21	"	Moved to Proven.	
"	22	"	Went to Heavy Mobile Workshop. Received visit from A.D.O.S. & I.O.M.	
"	23	"	Visited 88, 87 & 86 Bdes. also R. Fus. Lancs Fus & Mdx.	
"	24	"	Went to Bailleul	
"	25	"	Attended Q Conference of Staff Captains. Visited 88 Bde HQ, Essex, Hants, Worcesters, Newfoundland, Inniskillings & Borders.	
"	26	"	Went to Bailleul	
"	27	"	Visited D.D.O.S. & A.D.O.S.	
"	30	"	Visited Lancs. Fus. R. Fus. Dublin Fus & 86 Bde HQrs	
"	31	"	Visited Essex Hants Worcesters & Newfoundland. Recd. visit from A.D.O.S. Recd. 50 sets of packsaddlery	

H. Evans Capt
DADOS - 29 Divn
31.7.17

2449 Wt. W14957/M90 750,000 1/16 J.B.C. & A. Forms/C.2118/12.

Instructions regarding War Diaries and Intelligence Summaries are contained in F. S. Regs., Part II. and the Staff Manual respectively. Title pages will be prepared in manuscript.

WAR DIARY
or
~~INTELLIGENCE SUMMARY.~~
(Erase heading not required.)

Army Form C. 2118.

D.A.D.O.S.
Vol 14

Place	Date	Hour	Summary of Events and Information	Remarks and references to Appendices
PROVEN	21/7/17		Reveille 6 a.m. Breakfast 7.45 a.m. Inspection of Lines 9 a.m. Section Inspections. Cleaning limbers. Party warned for tour of duty of 2 days attached to Guards Divn in Trenches.	
			Rail transport from PROVEN – INTERNATIONAL CORNER at 21 hrs provided. Strength 4 officers 50 O.R. Reported to DMGO Guards DIVISION at INTERNATIONAL CORNER Ordered to report to O.C. 4 M.G. Coy. No work.	ST JULIEN Ed. 5A 1:10,000
PROVEN.	22/7/17		Church Parade 9.30 a.m. Church Army Tent PROVEN R.C. 10 a.m. S.W. Borderers Lines	
			Party in Trenches divided into 2 parties. One party for digging B11a5.6 one party night firing from B17a3.8. Considerable shelling during night with gas shells. No 4 M.G. Coy H.Q. A10b5.6.	ELVERDINGHE Ed 5A 1:10,000 / BELGIUM & FRANCE SHEET 28 1:40,000
PROVEN	23/7/17		Routine as usual. Orders to send relief of 4 officers & 50 men to 1st party. Order cancelled. Veterinary officer inspected mules & riding horses. 1 riding horse cast 2 for dipping against mange. Both parties carried out night firing.	
PROVEN.	24/7/17		24 Extra Packsaddles received. Practised putting on all gear including rations & water in afternoon. Relief party paraded 2.30 p.m met by 2 motor lorries to carry party to International Corner. Cancelled at 3 p.m. 2 officers 25 men returned 5 p.m.	

A5834 Wt W4973/M687 750,000 8/16 D. D. & L. Ltd. Forms/C.2118/13.

Instructions regarding War Diaries and Intelligence Summaries are contained in F. S. Regs., Part II. and the Staff Manual respectively. Title pages will be prepared in manuscript.

WAR DIARY

or

~~INTELLIGENCE SUMMARY.~~

(Erase heading not required.)

Army Form C. 2118.

Place	Date	Hour	Summary of Events and Information	Remarks and references to Appendices
PROVEN.	25/7/17.		Routine as usual. Practised Packing all gear on packsaddles. 2nd Party returned 2p.m. Remainder of Coy paid out on Monday 23-7-17 & each party paid out as they returned from trenches.	
			Strength officers 10 O.R 174. 1 loader with G.S. Wagon.	
			Riding 5 47 mules 2 H.D. with G S Wagon with Train	
			1 man slight accident sick.	
PROVEN.	26/7/17		Routine as usual. All transport animals inoculated against glanders. Orders received to send 4 officers & 50 men to be attached to 4th Guards M.G. Coy. ~~Parades 9 a m S O's Inspections. O C B~~ ~~10 a m Fire Direction with Sections by S.O's. 11-12 noon Combined Drill~~	
PROVEN	27/7/17		Orders received to send party with 8 guns & ammunition. Left 2.30 p m men by motor lorry & transport marching.	
			Parades 9 a m S O's Inspections	
			10 a m F. Direction with Sections	
			11-12 noon Combined Drill	
			2.15-3.15pm Fire Direction (Barrage) Officers & N C Os	
			3.15-4.15 Care & Cleaning.	

Instructions ~~regarding~~ War Diaries and Intelligence Summaries ~~are~~ contained in F. S. Regs., Part II. and the Staff Manual respectively. Title pages will be prepared in manuscript.

WAR DIARY

or

~~INTELLIGENCE~~ SUMMARY.

(Erase heading not required.)

Army Form C. 2118.

Place	Date	Hour	Summary of Events and Information	Remarks and references to Appendices
PROVEN	28/7/17		Report by orderly received 11 a.m from O.C party in ~~Trenches~~ line. Casualties by aircraft OR 3 killed 4 wounded. ~~[illegible]~~ Line pushed forward and M.G harassing fire carried out by party. Water sent up by petrol tins at 2.30 p.m. Limbers for bringing guns back to-morrow. Parades Rifle Inspections, Physical Training & Squad Drill.	
PROVEN.	29/7/17		Routine as usual. Party in trenches carried out night firing from same positions.	
PROVEN.	30/7/17		Parades. Inspections, Anti-gas Drill, Elementary Gun Drill, & Direction under Section Officers. Party returned 7 p.m – guns & limbers returned 1.45 a.m 30/31st. One section ordered to take over Guard of Ammunition Dump. Left 8.30 p.m.	
PROVEN.	31/7/17.		~~No~~ 1 Section to HARDINGE – guarding waterworks – left 3 p.m. ~~[illegible]~~ a Strength 10 Officers 160 O.R.	

Instructions regarding War Diaries and Intelligence Summaries are contained in F. S. Regs., Part II. and the Staff Manual respectively. Title Pages will be prepared in manuscript.

WAR DIARY

~~or~~

~~INTELLIGENCE SUMMARY~~

(Erase heading not required.)

Army Form C. 2118.

DADOS 29 D

August 1917

Vol 14

Place	Date	Hour	Summary of Events and Information	Remarks and references to Appendices
Proven	2	August	Visited Inniskilling Fusrs. S.W.B. + K.O.S.B. Recd 100 special Candle Carriers for trench artillery.	
"	4	"	Visited DADOS. Guards Division.	
"	6	"	Went to Dunkirk to purchase stores. 500 suits obtained specially from Calais by lorry for artillery.	
J Camp	8	"	Moved from Proven to J Camp. Recd visit from ADOS	
"	9	"	Went to Dunkirk to purchase Stores. Recd visit from DADOS 20th Div.	
"	10	"	Capt. Gibson attached for instruction. Visited 87 + 88 Bdes Dublin Fusrs. + Inniskillings	
"	13	"	Visited Dunkirk to purchase stores.	
"	14	"	Went to refilling point to observe & report on issue of Ordnance Stores.	
"	15	"	Recd visit from ADOS + DDOS. Went to XIV Corps Light workshops.	
"	17	"	Visited Units of 87 + 88 Bdes	
"	19	"	Recd. visit from ADOS.	
"	22	"	Visited Royals Dublin Fusrs, Mdx, Essex, Hants, Worcester, [illegible], + 88 Bde H.Qrs.	
"	24	"	Went to Proven to select site for new Dump. Visited various C.C.S's for [illegible]	
"	25	"	Visited 87 Bde H.Qrs., K.O.S.B., S.W.B., Inniskilling Fusrs, + Border Regt.	
"	26	"	Visited 88 Bde. H.Qrs. Recd visit from ADOS. XIV Corps.	
"	28	"	Visited CCS's + went to Proven. Recd visit from ADOS XIV Corps.	
Proven	29	"	Moved from J Camp to Proven	
"	31	"	Visited Calais in accordance with instructions from Fifth Army DDOS O/19/1/11 d 20/8/17.	

A. [illegible] Capt.

DADOS. 29 Div

4 9 17

2449 Wt. W14957/M90 750,000 1/16 J.B.C. & A. Forms/C.2118/12.

Vol 16

War Diary

From

1st September 1917

To

30th September 1917

D. A. D. O. S.

29th Division

Volume XXXI

Instructions regarding War Diaries and Intelligence Summaries are contained in F. S. Regs., Part II. and the Staff Manual respectively. Title Pages will be prepared in manuscript.

WAR DIARY
or
~~INTELLIGENCE SUMMARY~~
(Erase heading not required.)

Army Form C. 2118.

September 1917

Place	Date	Hour	Summary of Events and Information	Remarks and references to Appendices
Proven	2 September		Returned from visit to C.O.O. Calais	
"	3	"	Attended Administrative Staff Conference re Winter requirements.	
"	5	"	Visited 86th 87th & 88th Bdes.	
"	7	"	" XIV Corps Ordnance Workshops	
"	9	"	" 5th Army Gun Pk 86 Bde Bailleul & various C.C.S's.	
"	10	"	Went to Dunkirk. Artillery being specially re-equipped.	
"	11	"	Visited 86 Bde.	
"	12	"	Went to 5th Army Gun Park	
"	13	"	Went to Amiens	
"	17	"	Visited a D.O.S. XIV Corps, D.A.D.O.S. Guards Divn & various C.C.S's.	
"	20	"	Visited 88 Bde & site of new Dump @ I Camp	
"	21	"	Visited railhead at International Corner re unloading &c of 16000 blankets	
I Camp	22	"	Moved from Proven to I Camp.	
	24	"	Visited all the Inf Bdes & the 12 Battns.	
	26	"	Visited the 3 R.E. Field Coys.	
	27	"	Visited 8. C.C.S's to collect surplus Ordnance Stores &c	
	28	"	Visited 5th Army Gun Pk. Went to Bailleul. Supply of winter vests & drawers recd.	
	29	"	Visited a D.O.S. Lieut Bannerman attached as relief.	
	30	"	Visited workshops, Salvage, & Railhead.	

W.J. Jameson Capt. A.O.D.
A/D.A.D.O.S.
29th Division

1/10/17.

Instructions regarding War Diaries and Intelligence Summaries are contained in F. S. Regs., Part II. and the Staff Manual respectively. Title Pages will be prepared in manuscript.

WAR DIARY
or
~~INTELLIGENCE SUMMARY~~

(Erase heading not required.)

Army Form C. 2118.

DADOS 29 D October 1917

(32)

Vol 17

Place	Date	Hour	Summary of Events and Information	Remarks and references to Appendices
J Camp	1st October		Visited Corps H.Q. at Hazebrouck Local Purchase.	
"	2nd	"	Routine work.	
	3rd	"	To I.O.M. 11 & 12 Shops, Gun Park & two C.C.S's.	
	4th	"	} Routine work.	
	5th	"		
International Corner	6th	"	Moved office to Dump near International Corner A8 b4.4 Sheet 28 N.W.	
	7th	"	Went to H.Q. XIV Corps – A.D.O.S.	
	8th	"	To Calais – Local Purchase for A.D.O.S. Visited Ordnance re Horse Shoe Nails – Div Train	
	9th	"	Routine work	
	10th	"	Arrangements made for move to Central Camp, Proven. Visited new dump & three C.C.S's.	
Walton Rd.	11th	"	Moved to new dump at Sheet 27 E18 b4.2	
–	12th	"	} Routine work	
–	13th	"		
	14	"	Lieut Bannerman left Division. Capt: Erith resumed duties of D.A.D.O.S.	
Basseux	17	"	Moved to Basseux. Division transferred from Fifth to Third Army	
"	20	"	Visited 86 Bde H.Qrs & Units	
"	21	"	" 87 & 88 Bde H.Qrs & Units	
"	22	"	2nd Blankets recd & issued to Bdes. Visited Railhead	
"	23	"	Winter Clothing recd.	
"	25	"	Went to Amiens for Local Purchases	
"	26	"	Visited D.D.O.S. Third Army.	

Instructions regarding War Diaries and Intelligence Summaries are contained in F. S. Regs., Part II. and the Staff Manual respectively. Title Pages will be prepared in manuscript.

WAR DIARY
or
~~INTELLIGENCE SUMMARY~~
(Erase heading not required.)

Army Form C. 2118.

October 1917

Place	Date	Hour	Summary of Events and Information	Remarks and references to Appendices
Bassens	27	Oct.	Went to 29th Divl Depot Batt. ascertained general requirements	
	29	-	Attended conference at ADOS - VI Corps	
	30	-	Visited Artillery in Doullens Area	

[signature] Capt
DADOS. 29 Divn
1/11/17

2449 Wt. W14957/M90 750,000 1/16 J.B.C. & A. Forms/C.2118/12.

CONFIDENTIAL

Vol 18

War Diary

of

D. A. D. O. S., 29th Divn

1 – 11 – 17

to

30 – 11 – 17

–

Vol. XXXIII

Army Form C. 2118.

Instructions regarding War Diaries and Intelligence Summaries are contained in F. S. Regs., Part II. and the Staff Manual respectively. Title Pages will be prepared in manuscript.

WAR DIARY
~~or~~
~~INTELLIGENCE SUMMARY~~

(Erase heading not required.)

Vol 33

November 1917.

Place	Date	Hour	Summary of Events and Information	Remarks and references to Appendices
Bussu	1st Nov. 1917	–	Visited IOM No 6 Medium Mobile Workshops & DADOS 3rd Div.	
"	3rd	–	Visited Depot Battn.	
	4th	–	Went to IOM VI Corps Light Mobile Workshops re alters to Stokes Shells for Demonstration	
"	5th	–	Went to Amiens purchasing. Visited H.Q. Div Artillery	
	7th	–	Visited 87 Bde & Battns. Obtained the altered Stokes Shells from IOM No 13 Hy Light Mobile Workshops.	
	9th	–	Visited 86 & 88 Bde H.Q. Battns & M. G. Coy.	
	10th	–	Went to IOM VI Corps Light Workshops. 500 bags waterproof & 192 sets of [illegible]	
	12	–	Visited new oven with DAQMG. Interviewed ADOS III Corps.	
	14	–	Visited ADOS VI Corps	
	15	–	Went to Amiens to purchase stores. Sent stores to new Dump	
Moislains	17	–	Moved to Moislains in III Corps.	
"	18	–	Went to Sorel. Visited OO III Corps Troops	
Sorel	19	–	Moved to Sorel. Visited ADOS III Corps. Established advanced Armourers Shop at Villers Plouich	
"	20	–	Recd visit from ADOS III Corps & visited him. Successful advance made.	
"	21	–	Visited railhead at Fins & arranged delivery of Stores by 60 cm railway	
"	22	–	Visited Staff Captains of 86, 87 & 88 Bde.	
"	23	–	Received a visit from ADOS III Corps	
"	24	–	Visited ADOS & went to Peronne	
"	26	–	Visited advanced dump at Villers Plouich & 87 Bde at Marcoing	
"	29	–	Visited ADOS III Corps at Templeux la Fosse	
"	30	.	Enemy broke through at Gouzeaucourt. Packed up as much as possible on lorry & dispatched them to [illegible]. Went with whole detachment into trenches in front of Revelon Farm. Gouzeaucourt recaptured by Guards Division. Withdrew after 3 hours in the trenches with 2 men leaving 17 men in the trenches. Found that Dump had been partially looted but that Police had set a guard to prevent further looting	

[signature] Capt.
DADOS 29 Div.

2449 Wt. W14957/M90 750,000 1/16 J.B.C. & A. Forms/C.2118/12.

21

No.29 DIV. SUPPLY COLUMN

War Diary for the month of DECEMBER 1917.

Volumn No.21.

Instructions regarding War Diaries and Intelligence Summaries are contained in F. S. Regs., Part II. and the Staff Manual respectively. Title Pages will be prepared in manuscript.

WAR DIARY
or
~~INTELLIGENCE SUMMARY~~
(Erase heading not required.)

Army Form C. 2118.

D.A.D.O.S. 29 D.
December 1917
Vol ~~22~~ 19

Place	Date	Hour	Summary of Events and Information	Remarks and references to Appendices
Sorel	1 Dec 1917		Obtained authority to withdraw 3 men from the trenches. Ascertained that truck of stores sent to advance dump had been unable to reach its destination & had been sent back to Nurlu. Position as regards personnel 12 men at Sorel. 3 at Villers Plouich 1 at Bassana 14 in the line at Revelon Farm 8 on leave	
"	2 Dec 1917		15 Bde RHA lost all guns. Indent sent for 18 - 18 pdrs & 6 - 4.5 Hows	
	3	"	Visited railhead at Ytres & found 3 trucks there. Visited ADOS III Corps.	
Le Cauroy	5	"	Moved to Le Cauroy in IV Corps.	
"	6	"	Commenced refitting Division. Issues from S. Base stopped by Third Army & Indents transferred to N. Base	
"	7	"	Went to St Pol to purchase stores &c	
"	9	"	Recd visit from DDOS III Army	
"	10	"	" " ADOS IV Corps	
"	11	"	Visited 86 87 & 88 Bdes & Units ~~Warning Order~~	
"	14	"	Visited 1st Newfoundland Regt.	
HUCQUELIERS	18	"	Moved to HUCQUELIERS Railhead HESDIN	
	19	"	Visited refilling points, 20 tons of stores at railhead	
HESDIN	20	"	Moved to HESDIN with Divl Tn. DHQ HUCQUELIERS.	
	21	"	Went to Boulogne & obtained frost nails for horses	
	22	"	Issued stores to Units at refilling points.	
	23	"	Lorry caught fire & was extinguished in 15 minutes. No Ordnance Stores damaged.	
"	24	"	Artillery rejoined Division.	
"	27	"	~~Visited St Pol~~ &c	
"	28	"	Visited 87 Bde Border Inniskillings & No 3 Coy Divl Tn	
"	31	"	87 Bde moved & left Division	

[signature] Capt
DADOS 29 Divn
31/12/17

2449 Wt. W14957/M90 750,000 1/16 J.B.C. & A. Forms/C.2118/12.

Instructions regarding War Diaries and Intelligence Summaries are contained in F. S. Regs., Part II. and the Staff Manual respectively. Title pages will be prepared in manuscript.

WAR DIARY
or
INTELLIGENCE SUMMARY.
(*Erase heading not required.*)

Vol 17

Army Form C. 2118.

Place	Dec. Date 1917	Hour	Summary of Events and Information	Remarks and references to Appendices
In The Field	1	-	Twenty two Lorries drawing Supplies for Division from YTRES. Refilling Point NURLU.	
"	2	-	Twelve lorries returned from Third Army Troops Sup. Column. Thirty four lorries drawing supplies for Division	
"	3	-	Two additional lorries detailed to D.A.D.O.S. 29th Div.	
"	4	-	Two Saurer lorries returned to Unit from "C" Supply Column.	
"	5	-	Unit moved to FREVENT. Twelve lorries remain i/c Lieut Appleyard for feeding 29th Artillery. Workshop personnel & Lorry of "R" Siege Park handed over to 3rd Corps Siege Park.	
"	6	-	Drawing from FREVENT for Division less Artillery	
"	10	-	Unit attached to "D" Corps Supply Column	
"	13	-	One additional lorry detailed for Postal duties.	
"	14	-	No. 40276. Pte Thomas W. attd Workshops 29 D.S.C. ex 1st R. Dub. Fusiliers transferred to 1st Base M.T. Depot under authority D.A.G., G.H.Q. C.R. No. 38706/977/A. dated 27.11.17. 232nd A.F.A. Lorries transferred to No. 9. D.S.C.	

T2134. Wt. W708-776. 500000. 4/15. Sir J. C. & S.

Instructions regarding War Diaries and Intelligence Summaries are contained in F. S. Regs., Part II. and the Staff Manual respectively. Title pages will be prepared in manuscript.

WAR DIARY
or
INTELLIGENCE SUMMARY.
(Erase heading not required.)

Army Form C. 2118.

Place	Date DEC 1917	Hour	Summary of Events and Information	Remarks and references to Appendices
In the Field	17	-	Column moved to HESDIN.	
"	18	-	Drawing supplies for Division less Artillery from HESDIN Railhead.	
"	20	-	Unit attached to "X" Corps. Supply Column	
"	23	-	Twelve lorries feeding Div. Artillery rejoined Column.	
"	24	-	Drawing supplies for Division + Artillery from HESDIN Railhead	
"	25	-	Thaw restrictions imposed for one day by 29th Div. A.687/6. d/-25/12/17.	
"	28	-	Lieut. F Wilding departed on 14 days Leave to U. Kingdom.	
"	30	-	2/Lieut. J.W. Walker i/c 7 lorries proceeded with 87th Brigade to new Area.	

Army Form C. 2118.

DADOS 29 D
Vol 35
January 1918
Vol 20

Instructions regarding War Diaries and Intelligence Summaries are contained in F. S. Regs., Part II. and the Staff Manual respectively. Title Pages will be prepared in manuscript.

WAR DIARY
~~or~~
~~INTELLIGENCE SUMMARY~~
(Erase heading not required.)

Place	Date	Hour	Summary of Events and Information	Remarks and references to Appendices
HESDIN	2 Jan	1918	Visited WIZERNES and made arrangements for Stores workshops + offices there.	
WIZERNES	4	–	Moved from HESDIN to WIZERNES. Railhead St OMER.	
"	6	–	Visited 88 Bde + there also DDOS 4th Army at CASSEL.	
"	8	–	DADOS proceeded on leave. Capt. Wilson acting DADOS.	
"	9	–	Visited 86 Bde Units	
"	10	–	Visited 88 Bde Units	
"	11	–	Artillery Capt Thiembronne Area	
"	12	–	Suspended issues St Omer	
"	13	–	Artillery railhead moved to Wippenhoek	
"	14	–	Visited St Omer to buy Stores	
"	15	–	Visited DADOS 8th Divn re arranged for impending move	
"	16	–	Visited St Omer to buy stores	
"	18	–	Sent part of stores to new area. Reopened issues new railhead on 19/1/18	
Mersey Camp Vlamertinghe	19	–	Moved to new area. railhead Vlamertinghe	
	20	–	Visited OO 8th Corps troops who was acting ADOS. 8th Corps salvage dump 29th Ordnance reserve dump + several CCSs re obtaining revolvers etc	
–	24	–	Capt. Smith returned from leave + took over duties of DADOS.	
	25	–	Visited OO. 8th Corps troops, Reserve stores + Poperinghe + H.Q. Division	
Road Camp Vlamertinghe	27	–	Moved to Road Camp Vlamertinghe	
	30	–	Visited 86 Bde. Dump at Poperinghe + IOM 110 + 66 Light Workshops + drew 2 sample frames for carrying water tins on limbers.	

[signature] Capt

DADOS - 29 Division

1/2/18

2449 Wt. W14957/M90 750,000 1/16 J.B.C. & A. Forms/C.2118/12.

Army Form C. 2118.

D.A.D.O.S. 29 D

February 1918

Vol 21

Instructions regarding War Diaries and Intelligence Summaries are contained in F. S. Regs., Part II. and the Staff Manual respectively. Title Pages will be prepared in manuscript.

WAR DIARY
~~or~~
~~INTELLIGENCE SUMMARY~~

(Erase heading not required.)

Place	Date	Hour	Summary of Events and Information	Remarks and references to Appendices
Road Camp Vlamertinghe	3 Feb	1918	Visited Ordnance Store at Poperinghe, A.D.O.S. VIII Corps, O.O.M. 10 + 56 Light Mobile Workshops, H.Q. Divl. Tn. 15 Bde. R.H.A. and D.H.Q.	
	5	"	Visited 26 Battery R.F.A. + D.H.Q. re harness. Lisson + Sommerbury left the Division	
	6	"	Recd visit from A.D.O.S. VIII Corps	
	7	"	Visited D.A.D.O.S. 8th Division at Steenvoorde and arranged details of move. Inspected store at Poperinghe.	
	9	"	Arranged to move Armourers Shop on 10th. Stores + Office 11th	
STEENVOORDE	11	"	Moved to STEENVOORDE. Railhead WIPPENHOEK.	
	12	"	Visited railhead. Arranged for issue of stores in new area	
	14	"	Visited 86, 87 + 88 Bdes. and 2nd Hants. Inspected Q.M. Stores of 2nd Hants	
	17	"	Visited Railhead + 4th Army	
	18	"	Visited 89th Fd. Amblce. Inspected Q.M. Stores.	
	20	"	Visited O.O. VIII Corps Troops, railhead + K.O.S.B.	
	23	"	Inspected Camp Commdt. Qmr. Stores.	
	24	"	Visited transport of 10th Innis Killing Fus. Visited 86 Bde. R.G.L.I. + Railhead	
	25	"	New War Establishment for Machine Gun Battn.	
	28	"	Visited 8th E. Lancs transport.	

[signature] Capt.
D.A.D.O.S. 29 Div.

1/3/18

2449 Wt. W14957/M90 750,000 1/16 J.B.C. & A. Forms/C.2118/12.

War Diary

DADOS 29 Div

1–31 March
1918.

Vol. 37

Instructions regarding War Diaries and Intelligence Summaries are contained in F. S. Regs., Part II. and the Staff Manual respectively. Title Pages will be prepared in manuscript.

WAR DIARY ~~or~~ ~~INTELLIGENCE~~ SUMMARY

(*Erase heading not required.*)

Army Form C. 2118.

Vol 37

March 1918

Place	Date	Hour	Summary of Events and Information	Remarks and references to Appendices
STEENVOORDE	2 March		All Lewis Guns recd	
"	4	-	Attended conference at ADOS VIII Corps. Visited railhead & DADOS 8th Div	
Road Camp VLAMERTINGHE	6	-	Moved from Steenvoorde to Vlamertinghe. Railhead Vlamertinghe. Took over stores in Poperinghe from 8th Division.	
	7	-	Arrival of new Dischargers Cups for Rifle Grenades	
	9	-	Visited Stores at Poperinghe 86 & 88 Bdes also Q Branch.	
	14	-	Visited DHQ Stores at Poperinghe. Went to St Omer to purchase stores. Checked QM Stores DAC.	
	15	-	Lectured DAC & 17 Bde RFA on Economy in Stores	
	16	-	Checked QM Stores 17 Bde RFA.	
	17	-	1 Lewis gun demanded for R. Nfld. Regt	
Dirty Bucket Camp VLAMERTINGHE	20	-	Shell burst in Ordnance Dump. One hut entirely destroyed. Corpl. Prestner killed 2 men wounded evacuated, 3 others bruised suffering from shock returned to duty. Moved to new dump at Dirty Bucket Camp.	
"	26	-	Visited store at Poperinghe, Gun Park, OO VIII Corps Troops & DADOS 33rd Division	
"	28	-	Drew reserve of clothing from OO VIII Corps Troops.	
"	29	-	Visited Division Store at Poperinghe & D.O.M.	

[signature] Capt

DADOS 29 Div

3/4/18

2449 Wt. W14957/M90 750,000 1/16 J.B.C. & A. Forms/C.2118/12.

Instructions regarding War Diaries and Intelligence Summaries are contained in F. S. Regs., Part II. and the Staff Manual respectively. Title Pages will be prepared in manuscript.

WAR DIARY
~~or~~
~~INTELLIGENCE~~ SUMMARY

(Erase heading not required.)

Army Form C. 2118.

DADOS 31st D[illegible] 39 D
April 1918.
23

Place	Date	Hour	Summary of Events and Information	Remarks and references to Appendices
Dirty Bucket Camp VLAMERTINGHE	3rd April		Visited DHQ & Store at Poperinghe. Went C.C.S's collecting rifles.	
	5th April		Visited 2nd Army School of Sniping & drew 30 sniper rifles & 3 rifles fitted with telescopic sights.	
	7	-	Visited DHQ & Store at Poperinghe. Arranged to store surplus stores. Issues suspended.	
	8	-	Visited DADOS. 41st Divn & arranged handing over of stores. Transferred Artillery to 41st Divn	
	9	-	Final preparations for move. Wired Calais accept 11/4/17. Re-indented on Gun Park No 1.	
LE PARC	10	-	Moved to Le Parc. Divl HQ. Les Lauriers. Issues stopped from Base. In XV Corps First Army.	
MORBECQUE	11	-	Moved to Morbecque. Division moved to La Motte. No Office. Stores in Lorries	
CAESTRE	12	-	Moved to Caestre. Division moved to Caestre. No Office. Stores on Lorries. Second Army.	
St SYLVESTRE	14	-	Moved to St. Sylvestre Cappel with Division. Opened Office and Store. Wired Calais accept.	
			Gun Park moved to Watten. 38th Divl. Artillery attached.	
	15	-	Refitting Division. 73 Lewis Guns demanded. 3 Lorries sent to Calais for Stores. 3 Lorries sent to Gun Park at WATTEN.	
	16	-	Refitting Division. 43 Lewis & 1 Vickers Gun received. 1 Lorry sent to Gun Park.	
	17	-	Refitting Division. 30 Lewis guns received. Lorry sent to Calais for [illegible] [illegible] bicycles. Recd [illegible] from ADOS XV Corps	
	18	-	Issued to Lewis guns to 88th Bde. Visited 88th Bde. [illegible].	
HONDEGHEM	19	-	Moved to Hondeghem.	
	21	-	Visited 87 Bde	
	22	-	Lorry sent to Calais to get Stores for 87 Bde. visited 86 Bde	
	23	-	Lorry sent to Calais to get Stores for 87 Bde. visited 88 Bde & Units	
	26	-	Two Lorries sent to Calais for equipment. Visited ADOS XV Corps at WARDRECQUES. Arranged with DADOS	
			31st Division move to WALLON-CAPPEL.	
WALLON CAPPEL	28	.	Moved to WALLON-CAPPEL Railhead EBBLINGHEM	
	29	-	Lorry sent to Calais for Clothing for gassed men & for hot food containers	
	30	.	Visited 86, 87 & 88 Bdes. [illegible] of 88 Bde. Belts for Vickers Guns increased to 32 per gun.	

[signature] Capt
DADOS 29 Divn.

1/5/18.

2449 Wt. W14957/M90 750,000 1/16 J.B.C. & A. Forms/C.2118/12.

Instructions regarding War Diaries and Intelligence Summaries are contained in F. S. Regs., Part II. and the Staff Manual respectively. Title pages will be prepared in manuscript.

WAR DIARY

~~or~~

~~INTELLIGENCE SUMMARY.~~

(Erase heading not required.)

DADOS 29 D

Army Form C. 2118.

May 1918.

Vol 24

Place	Date	Hour	Summary of Events and Information	Remarks and references to Appendices
WALLON CAPPEL	2 May	–	Visited Gun Park, O.O. Corps Troops + Ordnance Workshops. Collected ammunition weights for Vickers Guns but failed to obtain Knobkerries	
	3	–	Railhead moved to WARDRECQUES	
	6	–	Visited 19th Divl Artillery re refitting + ADOS XV Corps. 2 lorries returned from Calais with special stores.	
	8	–	Went to Calais to obtain Dischargers + dummy 36 grenades for 87 Bde. Also arranged about scythes for S.S.O.	
	9	–	Visited 87th Bde	
	10	–	Went to St Omer + purchased torch refills.	
	11	–	Visited 89 Field Ambulance	
	13	–	Moved 19th Artillery to 79th Division	
	14	–	Recd visit from ADOS XV Corps.	
	15	–	Visited Worcesters + Leinsters inspected Lewis guns also visited 88 Bde H.Qrs	
	16	–	Inspected Quartermaster's stores of Lancashire Fusiliers	
	17	–	Inspected Quartermaster's stores of Royal Dublin Fusiliers	
	20	–	Inspected Quartermaster's Stores of S.W.B.	
	23	–	Inspected Quartermaster's Stores of Worcesters.	
	24	–	Visited ADOS + D.O.M.	
	30	–	Inspected Quartermaster's Stores of Hants	

[signature] Capt
DADOS 29 Divn
31/5/18.

A7092 Wt. W12839/M1293 750,000. 1/17. D. D & L., Ltd. Forms/C2118/14.

7

Instructions regarding War Diaries and Intelligence Summaries are contained in F. S. Regs., Part II. and the Staff Manual respectively. Title pages will be prepared in manuscript.

WAR DIARY

~~or~~

~~INTELLIGENCE SUMMARY.~~

(*Erase heading not required.*)

Army Form C. 2118.

DADOS June 1918 29 D

Vol 25

Place	Date	Hour	Summary of Events and Information	Remarks and references to Appendices
WALLON CAPPEL	1	June	Inspected Qmrs Stores of 2nd Leinster Regt	
	3	–	Visited No 2 Heavy Mobile Workshop + ADOS XV Corps.	
	5	–	Inspected Qmrs Stores of 460 Battery + Warwick Battery. Drew 10 Lewis Gun AA Mtgs Jackson Tripod pattern.	
			Demanded 72 Lewis guns to bring Division up to 28 guns per Battn.	
	6	–	72 Lewis guns drawn from Gun Park. New Armourer for 2nd Leinsters reported.	
	10	–	Visited I.O.M. No 2 Heavy Mobile [illegible] to draw [illegible]	
	12	–	Drew 50 No 30 Periscopes. Recd 45 Carriers Lewis Gun. Golf Bag Pattern	
	14	–	Inspected Qmrs Stores of 2nd Royal Fusrs.	
	15	–	Visited ADOS XV Corps also S.O.S School 2nd Army at LUMBRES obtained 20 rifles fitted with Telescopic Sights + 2 Sniper Rifles. Drew 8 Tarpaulins from Corps.	
	17	–	Inspected Qmrs. Stores of B Battery + L. Battery. Received 70 Fly Sprayers from Base	
	19	–	6 Monkey Puzzle mountings drawn from Corps.	
	20	–	Orders for move received. Visited DADOS 31st Divn + new Area.	
	21	–	88th Bde moved to LUMBRES. Arranged to issue stores in new Area at refilling points	
WARDRECQUES	22	–	Moved to WARDRECQUES. 31st Division relieved 29th Division in the line.	
–	23	–	Delivery of stores at refilling points commenced. Lewis Guns of 1st Border Regt. called in for overhaul.	
			Visited 88th Bde and 2nd Army School of Sniping. 36 Lewis guns drawn to complete Battns to 36.	
	24	–	Recd a visit from ADOS XV Corps	
	26	–	86th Bde moved up in support. Stores being issued at DADOS 31st Division Dump at WALLON CAPPEL	
	27	–	Visited 88 Bde.	
	30	–	Ninety Jute nosebags received for issue on trial.	

H. Brown Major
DADOS. 29 Divn
30/6/18

A7092 Wt. W12839/M1293 750,000. 1/17. D. D & L., Ltd. Forms/C2118/14.

Instructions regarding War Diaries and Intelligence Summaries are contained in F. S. Regs., Part II. and the Staff Manual respectively. Title pages will be prepared in manuscript.

WAR DIARY
or
~~INTELLIGENCE SUMMARY.~~
(Erase heading not required.)

Army Form C. 2118.

D A D O S 29 D
Vol. 41
July 1918

Place	Date	Hour	Summary of Events and Information	Remarks and references to Appendices
WARDRECQUES	1 July		Visited 87 Bde, Borders + SWB's. Jute Nose Bags issued for trial + report.	
"	2	"	Visited 86 Bde.	
"	5	"	Visited Dublin Fus + L Battery. Went to Blaringhem + arranged with Sanitary Officer to borrow latrine buckets etc for horseshows.	
"	7	"	4 Tug of War ropes authorised by Army for training purposes.	
"	9	"	Divisional Horse Show.	
"	12	"	1st Border Regt moved up to N. of Hazebrouck	
"	13	"	Visited Railhead. 4 extra Lewis Guns authorised for each Field Coy RE.	
"	15	"	Lewis Guns for Field Coys RE received. Visited Leinsters + Hants. 87 Bde in the line	
"	16	"	Orders recd for 87 Bde to be relieved on 19th. 29th Division placed in Army Reserve	
"	17	"	Visited 86 Bde.	
"	18	"	Lewis Guns for Artillery Batteries increased from 2 to 4 per battery. Indent forwarded	
"	19	"	88th Bde moved from LUMBRES Area to BLARINGHEM Area.	
"	20	"	Visited 87 Bde + Units also Hants + Worcesters	
"	21	"	16 Lewis guns received for Artillery. 3 Light German machine guns sent in by 1st R. Dublin Fus.	
BAVINCHOVE	22	"	Moved to CASSEL and then to BAVINCHOVE	
"	23	"	Stores issued at refilling point to 86 + 88 Bdes + Artillery	
"	24	"	In X Corps (HQ ZUYTPEENE)	
"	25	"	230 Trench Shelters drawn from OO X Corps Troops	
"	26	"	Visited 86 87 + 88 Bdes. Stores moved into a barn	
"	27	"	Visited ADOS X Corps at ZUYTPEENE	
"	30	"	Warning of move received	
"	31		Visited DADOS 1st Australian Division + arranged to take over dump at EBBLINGHEM. Visited ADOS XV Corps	

1/8/18. [signature] Major
DADOS 29 Div.

A7092 Wt W12839/M1293 750,000. 1/17. D. D & L., Ltd. Forms/C2118/14.

DADOS 29 D
Vol. 42
Aug. 1918

Army Form C. 2118.

Instructions regarding War Diaries and Intelligence Summaries are contained in F. S. Regs., Part II. and the Staff Manual respectively. Title pages will be prepared in manuscript.

WAR DIARY
or
~~INTELLIGENCE SUMMARY.~~
(Erase heading not required.)

WO 27

Place	Date	Hour	Summary of Events and Information	Remarks and references to Appendices
BAVINCHOVE	1 Aug.		Units commence to take over from 1st Australian Division	
Near Les Cinq Rues	3	"	Moved Ordnance dump to V 24 c 6.9 near Les Cinq Rues. D.H.Q. moved to near St Sylvestre Cappel.	
			Took over Area & Trench Stores from 1st Australian Division	
	4	"	100 Oilskin Combination Suits for Mustard Gas received.	
	7	"	Visited 87 Bde H.Q. & Inspected Qmrs. Stores also visited 1st Border Regt.	
	8	"	8 Tons of stores received & 1 water cart for the Div B's.	
	9	"	Visited D.H.Q. and Div'l Salvage Dump.	
	11	"	Visited ADOS. XV Corps	
	12	"	Recd. visit from ADOS XV Corps	
	14	"	Visited Corps Salvage & 2nd Army SOS School re rifles fitted with Telescopic Sights.	
	18	"	Attended conference at ADOS XV Corps.	
	19	"	Successful attack by 29th Divn in conjunction with 9th Divn	
	23	"	Visited Sniping school. Obtained 6 rifles. Inspected Transport for Corps Horse Show	
			Visited railhead & received visit from DDOS Second Army	
	25	"	Inspected Shoemakers Tailors Shops &c of 2 Royal Fusiliers	
	27	"	Visited Railhead, Div'l Ammn Dump, Baths Offr 1/2 Monmouths & Salvage Offr also Corps Salvage Dump.	
	29	"	D HQ moved to BORRE.	
	30	"	Visited Corps Salvage & 453 W Riding R.E. Coy. Inspected Ordnance Stores	

H. ..... Major
DADOS. 29th Division
31/8/18

A7092 Wt W1285 9/M1293 750,000. 1/17. D. D & L., Ltd. Forms/C2118/14.

Instructions regarding War Diaries and Intelligence Summaries are contained in F. S. Regs., Part II. and the Staff Manual respectively. Title pages will be prepared in manuscript.

WAR DIARY

~~or~~

~~INTELLIGENCE SUMMARY.~~

(Erase heading not required.)

Army Form C. 2118.

DADOS

Vol 43

September 1918

28

Place	Date	Hour	Summary of Events and Information	Remarks and references to Appendices
Mons-les-Cing Rues	1	Sep	Attended Conference at XV Corps. Arranged to move to Hazebrouck.	
HAZEBROUCK	2	"	Moved to Hazebrouck. Arranged to issue stores at refilling points.	
	3	"	Issued stores at refilling points.	
	4	"	Visited Railhead at Hazebrouck Garage.	
~~FLETRE~~	5	"	Arranged to move to Ionic House. Visited Bdes	
nr FLETRE	7	"	Moved to Ionic House. Railhead changed to BAILLEUL. Major Fowler went on leave Capt Wilson acting as DADOS	
HAZEBROUCK	11	"	Moved to Hazebrouck. Railhead changed to Hazebrouck Garage.	
	12	"	Visited units of 86th & 88th Brigades.	
	16	"	arranged for move to WATOU.	
	17	"	Railhead moved to Rousbrugge	
			Moved to Watou. Border Camp	
WATOU	18	"	Railhead moved to International Corner	
	21	"	Major Fowler returned from leave	
	22	"	Visited DHQ. Went to Calais to draw special stores	
	25	"	Visited DHQ 86 Bde 15 HA Section re special stores & move	
	27	"	Moved to Brake Camp. Stores moved to Planet light	
BRAKE Camp	28	"	DHQ moved to YPRES	
	29	"	1000 magazines L.G. obtained from II Corps. Two new lorries from demanded to replace casualties	
	30	"		

A.H. Fowler Major
DADOS 29 Div.

Army Form C. 2118.

WAR DIARY
or
~~INTELLIGENCE SUMMARY.~~
(Erase heading not required.)

Instructions regarding War Diaries and Intelligence Summaries are contained in F. S. Regs., Part II. and the Staff Manual respectively. Title pages will be prepared in manuscript.

Vol 44
October 1918

DADVS 29 Div

Place	Date	Hour	Summary of Events and Information	Remarks and references to Appendices
BRAKE CAMP	1	Oct.	Two Lewis Guns received.	
	2	"	Went to Gun Park re isolated SAA Section	
	3	"	Division to be withdrawn from the line.	
	4	"	Division out of the line. Refitting commenced.	
	5	"	Visited 87 Bde	
	6	"	Visited Comforts of Div Tr. and MVS.	
VLAMERTINGHE	7	"	Moved to Vlamertinghe Division moved to Ypres	
	9	"	Went IOM No 4 Heavy Mobile Workshops to get sample T Barrow	
	12	"	Visited Gun Park to get urgent battle stores	
YPRES	13	"	Moved to Ypres Office & stores remaining at Vlamertinghe	
MOLENHOEK	15	"	Moved with Office & Stores to Molenhoek Advance continues	
LEDEGHEM	16	"	Moved to Ledeghem. Railhead St Jean	
	18	"	6 Lewis Guns demanded 9 G.S. limbers arrived for SAA Section.	
	19	"	Railhead moved to PASSCHENDAELE	
nr COURTRAI	21	"	Moved to near Courtrai. Issues suspended.	
	23	"	Division being relieved tonight by 41st Division Visited 88 Bde Issues resumed	
	24	"	Railhead moved to BEYTHEM Refitting Division. Visited 86 + 87 Bdes	
	25	"	Move to XV Corps Area commenced	
MOUVEAUX	27	"	Moved to Mouveaux Railhead remains at Beythem	
	28	"	Visited H.Q. Div Artillery & discussed question of refitting	
	29	"	Visited ADVS XV Corps Railhead Armentieres	
	30	"	Cleared Vlamertinghe Dump.	

[signature] Major
DADVS. 29th Division

2/11/18

A7092 Wt W12839/M1293 750,000. 1/17. D. D & L., Ltd. Forms/C2118/14.

Instructions regarding War Diaries and Intelligence Summaries are contained in F. S. Regs., Part II. and the Staff Manual respectively. Title pages will be prepared in manuscript.

WAR DIARY ~~or~~ ~~INTELLIGENCE SUMMARY.~~

(Erase heading not required.)

Army Form C. 2118.

DADOS 29 D
Vol 45
November 1918
30

Place	Date	Hour	Summary of Events and Information	Remarks and references to Appendices
MOUVEAUX	1 November		Railhead moved to LA MADELEINE (nr LILLE). Visited Railhead. 2nd Blanket arrived.	
	2	-	Sent to S.O.S. School at BOURNONVILLE for Sniper Rifles & 3 Lewis guns for Leinsters received from Gun Park. One 18 pdr gun drawn by L Battery.	
	3	-	Winter horse shoes being issued	
	5	-	Visited COURTRAI Clothing Depot	
	6	-	Warned to prepare for move to X Corps.	
ROLLEGHEM	7	-	Moved to Rolleghem. Railhead remain at La Madeleine	
	8	-	Visited railhead. Packsaddlery & water carriers being drawn from O.O X Corps Tps & O.O II Army Troops No 1.	
St GENOIS	10	-	Office moved to St Genois. Dump remains at Rolleghem. Railhead still La Madeleine	
	11	-	Armistice in force at 11 a.m. Stores being moved from Rolleghem to St Genois.	
	12	-	Stores moved to St Genois	
RENAIX	14	-	Moved to Renaix. Stores still at St Genois. Railhead ~~Sweveghem~~ Sweveghem	
FLOBECQ	15	-	Office and stores moved to Flobecq. Transferred to II Corps.	
ENGHIEN	18	-	Moved to Enghien. Railhead Vichte.	
TUBIZE	21	-	Moved to Tubize. A.D.O.S at Lessines.	
	22	-	Railhead Oudenarde	
BRAINE L'ALLEUD	23	-	Moved to Braine L'Alleud	
OTTIGNIES	24	-	Moved to Ottignies. Horse shoes received. Stores issued at refilling points.	
NIL ABBESSE	25	-	Moved to Nil Abbesse. Horse shoes issued	
GRAND-ROSIERE	27	-	Moved to Grand Rosiere.	
HUY	28	-	Moved to Huy	
ANTHISNES	30	-	Moved to Anthisnes. Boots & clothing issued	

[illegible] Major
DADOS 29 Div

A7092 Wt. W12839/M1293 750,000. 1/17. D. D & L., Ltd. Forms/C2118/14.

Instructions regarding War Diaries and Intelligence Summaries are contained in F. S. Regs., Part II. and the Staff Manual respectively. Title pages will be prepared in manuscript.

WAR DIARY
or
~~INTELLIGENCE~~ SUMMARY.
(Erase heading not required.)

Army Form C. 2118.

DADOS 29 D
December 1918
V.D. 31

Place	Date	Hour	Summary of Events and Information	Remarks and references to Appendices
SPRIMONT	1 December		Moved to Sprimont. Visited railhead at AMAY.	
NIVEZE	2	–	Moved to Niveze. Railhead PEPINSTER	
MALMEDY	4	–	Entered Germany. Moved to Malmedy. Railhead ROTGEN.	
KALTERHERBERG	5	–	Moved to Kalterherberg. Truck of horseshoes & winter clothing arrived at railhead	
KESTERNICH	6	–	Moved to Kesternich	
ZULPICH	7	–	Moved to Zulpich. Railhead DUREN	
EFFEREN	8		Moved to Efferen	
	9	–	DHQ moved to Hermulheim. Refitting commenced. Railhead HORREM.	
	10	–	DHQ moved to Sulz. Ordnance remain at Efferen. 4000 prs of boots received.	
	13	–	DHQ moved to Bensberg. Railhead ERHENFELD.	
BENSBERG	14	–	Railhead BERG GLADBACH. Moved to Bensberg	
	15	–	Received visit from ADOS II Corps	
	17	–	Visited railhead.	
SAND	21	–	Moved to Sand	
ODENTHAL	22	–	Moved to Odenthal	
	24	–	3rd Blanket authorised.	
	28	–	1st RAOC man demobilized	
	29	–	Amended arrangement for issue of stores owing to move of 87 Bde & Ammunition	

[signature] Major RAOC
DADOS 29 Divn

A7092 Wt. W12839/M1293 750,000. 1/17. D. D & L., Ltd. Forms/C2118/14.

RHINE ARMY
SOUTHERN DIVISION
LATE 29TH DIVISION

DEP. ASST DIR. ORDNANCE SERVICES
JAN - OCT 1919

~~2069~~ 2070 ✓ 2084

Instructions regarding War Diaries and Intelligence Summaries are contained in F. S. Regs., Part II. and the Staff Manual respectively. Title pages will be prepared in manuscript.

WAR DIARY

~~or~~

~~INTELLIGENCE SUMMARY.~~

(Erase heading not required.)

Army Form C. 2118.

~~24~~ Vol 47

January 1919

32

Place	Date	Hour	Summary of Events and Information	Remarks and references to Appendices
ODENTHAL	1	1919 January	Major H. Brown went on 30 days leave. Captain R. Wilson took over the duties as D.A.D.O.S.	
	2/25	Jany.	Usual Routine.	
	25	Jany	Captain R. Wilson went on leave. Lieut. D.B. MacNicol took over the duties of D.A.D.O.S.	

[illegible signature] Major

DADOS 29 Div

11/3/19

A7092. Wt. W12839/M1293. 750,000. 1/17. D. D & L., Ltd. Forms/C2118/14.

Instructions regarding War Diaries and Intelligence Summaries are contained in F. S. Regs., Part II. and the Staff Manual respectively. Title pages will be prepared in manuscript.

WAR DIARY

or

~~INTELLIGENCE SUMMARY.~~

(Erase heading not required.)

D.A.D.O.S.

Vol 48

February 1919

Army Form C. 2118.

33

Place	Date	Hour	Summary of Events and Information	Remarks and references to Appendices
	1919			
ODENTHAL	5 February		Major Brodie DADOS returned from leave	
	7	"	Conference with Div. Commander, & 38 Bde R.F.A. re supply of brill stores to	
	8	"	Visited ADOS I Corps & OO Corps Troops	
	10	"	Conference with 15 & 17 Bdes R.F.A.	
	11	"	Conference with DAC	
	12	"	Obtained 1000 substitute leather soles owing to shortage of [illegible]	
	14	"	Visited Cologne & requisitioned wire for caps. Visited ADOS I Corps	
	17	"	Collected wire from Cologne & visited ADOS I Corps	
	19	"	Instructed loads of stores read & Boots Dubbing to be obtained from New Zealand Division	
	20	"	Received warning that 2nd Hants Regt & 1/2 Monmouth Regt are leaving Division	
	23	"	One truck received at Burscheid. Embargo on returning old stores to Base removed	
	24	"	Orders of stores arrived at Burscheid.	
	25	"	Visited 87 Bde. Selected site at Burscheid for I.C.S. ADOS I Corps visited me	
	26	"	Collected clothing from Army	
	27	"	Truck arrived at railhead. Collecting more clothing from OO I Army Tps OO Cologne & DADOS New Zealand Division	

2/3/19.

H. Brodie Major
DADOS 29 Div.

A7092 Wt W128;9/M1293 750,000. 1/17. D. D & L., Ltd. Forms/C2118/14.

Instructions regarding War Diaries and Intelligence Summaries are contained in F. S. Regs., Part II. and the Staff Manual respectively. Title pages will be prepared in manuscript.

WAR DIARY
or
~~INTELLIGENCE SUMMARY.~~
(Erase heading not required.)

DADOS, Southern Div, Army of Rhine
Vol 51 May 1919

SECRET

Army Form C. 2118.

Place	Date	Hour	Summary of Events and Information	Remarks and references to Appendices
	1919			
ODENTHAL	3 May		Received visit from ADOS II Corps. Major Beavan arrived to take over duties of DADOS	
	4	"	Received a visit from the Divisional Commander	
	5	"	Visited Rautherod & Cologne	
	7	"	Received visit from the ADOS. Interviewed Div. Commander. Major Beavan proceeded on leave.	
	8	"	Visited Ohligs & Cologne on requisition duties	
	9	"	Visited Cologne on requisition duties	
	10	"	Cologne " "	
	14	"	Cologne " "	
	16	"	Ohligs " "	
	22	"	Attended conference at DHQ re arrangements in the event of an advance	
	23	"	Major Beavan returned from leave & took over duties of DADOS.	
	24		Visited M.G. Bn & inspected repairable transport with representative sent by [illegible]. 13 complete [illegible] wagons inspected - 1 condemned, 5 [illegible] & 2 [illegible] ordered to be sent to [illegible] for repair & 20 wheels condemned.	
	25		Arranged to accept winter clothing, blankets & [illegible] from 1/5 Borders to-day (Sunday) as sent [illegible] to [illegible] posts on Monday. All winter clothing & blankets to be accepted from units & sent by [illegible] lorries to [illegible] as soon as possible.	
	26		Instructions received from ADOS as to making up Anti-gas reserves - reserve of [illegible] gas & components to be drawn ~~[illegible]~~ on orders being received to move forward - ~~[illegible] arranged~~ [illegible] instructed by Corps to hand over to me 2 lorries for carrying these reserves - Procedure for [illegible] of [illegible] & [illegible]. [illegible] Anti gas [illegible] [illegible] forward detailed in ADOS letter.	
	27		Similar instruction recd in "G" Admin. Inst. Major [illegible] left for [illegible]. Visited Cologne & [illegible] balance of Maps & [illegible] from Requisition Bureau of some outstanding [illegible] orders.	

Instructions regarding War Diaries and Intelligence Summaries are contained in F. S. Regs., Part II. and the Staff Manual respectively. Title pages will be prepared in manuscript.

WAR DIARY
or
INTELLIGENCE SUMMARY.
(*Erase heading not required.*)

Army Form C. 2118.

Place	Date	Hour	Summary of Events and Information	Remarks and references to Appendices
OBERNTHAL, GERMANY	28		Visited Cologne & hastened Requisition Office for delivery of balance of nimps of plates [illegible] in my old requisition – 1000 plates promised for 29th. Visited ADOS at II Corps HQ & [illegible] asked if [illegible] Arty Units who are remaining could make up their deficiency equipment from that of disbanded units – ADOS agreed to this as these stores are not to be handed into Ordnance yet. Informed Staff Capt RA.	
	29	9 a.m. Routine work	Visited 6th & saw A.P.&S.S. [illegible] & give unofficial help in checking & packing up equipment of disbanded units. I must not take over these stores officially.	
	30		Visited Cologne & returned cash balance of Imprest a/c £120 to Field Cashier 2nd Army – money in future to be drawn from Paymaster, Cologne. All winter clothing & 3rd Blanket now handed in by units & returned to I.C.S.	
	31.		Visited 3 Bns & Bde HQ of 3rd Infty Bde & took notes of their particular requirements – took action on these notes on my return. Visited 29 MGBn re their complaint as to bad quality of [illegible] leather equipment recently issued to them. Unfortunately no samples were in stock for my inspection. Arranged to watch next receipts from Base & to tell the C.O. if the quality is really bad as stated by MGBn. 16 R.G.A. men reported for instruction in Ordnance duties from the Corps I.C.S. – no clerks among them – & no NCOs sent. These men are to be trained as storemen & if suitable will replace releasable Ordnance personnel.	

[signature]
Major..
D.A.D.O.S.
Southern Divn
31/5/19

A7092 Wt. W12839/M1293 750,000. 1/17. D. D & L., Ltd. Forms/C2118/14.

Instructions regarding War Diaries and Intelligence Summaries are contained in F. S. Regs., Part II. and the Staff Manual respectively. Title pages will be prepared in manuscript.

WAR DIARY
or
~~INTELLIGENCE SUMMARY.~~
(Erase heading not required.)

SECRET

Army Form C. 2118.

D.A.D.O.S Southern Div

Place	Date	Hour	Summary of Events and Information	Remarks and references to Appendices
Odenthal, Germany	1.		16 R.G.A. Gunners reported from DO II Corps. ICS for training as Storemen & clerks to relieve releasable RAOC personnel – Inspected these men & reviewed their documents – all tradesmen in civil life & none of them suitable as clerks – As only 3 RAOC Storemen are releasable – 16 is far too large a number. *	
	2.		Visited Railhead, Berg Gladbach – Found all correct & Sergt Sherwood returned from leave to take charge. Took requisition for Fly Sprayers & Beds for 16 Gunners to Staff Capt "Q" Cont Admn. Berg Gladbach for immediate provision to be made.	
	3.		Lorries fully engaged all day on various collecting & delivery work. Unable to draw Petrol Tins from MT Coy as instructed by "Q" :. asked MT Coy to deliver to me for issue – Orders received to find & instruct understudies for all 1914 & 1915 – RAOC men as early as possible to ensure release of 1914 men by 15th June, 1919.	
	4.		ADOS II Corps visited Office – Informed him I only required 9 ~~[illegible]~~ Gunners, at the outside, 6 for Store to understudy releasable Storemen & 3 for Railhead to release releasable ~~for~~ R.A.O.C. personnel – Confirmed this by letter. He informed me that the release of releasable men is being ~~[illegible]~~ treated separately – 60 releasable men are being sent from France when they can be spared. Great difficulty experienced by D.O.S in obtaining suitable clerks to understudy RAOC Clerks ~~[illegible]~~	
	5.		Sent Latrine Buckets, Hurricane lanterns, cups & plates & Camp kettles to Race ~~course~~ on loan for Div Race meeting. Informed ADOS that 6 of the fatigue men attached to me had volunteered for transfer to the RAOC to replace releasable Storemen – forwarded nominal roll & asked if they could be accepted in lieu of the Gunners, who are insubordinate & unwilling to learn.	

A7092 Wt. W12839/M1293 750,000. 1/17. D. D & L., Ltd. Forms/C2118/14.

Instructions regarding War Diaries and Intelligence Summaries are contained in F. S. Regs., Part II. and the Staff Manual respectively. Title pages will be prepared in manuscript.

WAR DIARY
or
INTELLIGENCE SUMMARY.
(Erase heading not required.)

Army Form C. 2118.

Place	Date	Hour	Summary of Events and Information	Remarks and references to Appendices
ODENTHAL GERMANY.	6th		General Routine work – Race meeting opened – Tentage [illegible] Flags & Flats Muslin & Bunting – Camp Kettles Soyer Stoves – Towels & sponges etc. [illegible] obtained from various sources & issued to [illegible] at Racecourse during preceding days.	
	7		General Routine work – 2nd day of Races – Sent 50% of my staff including attached to Races.	
	8		General Routine work. Tentage of 53 Marquees & A Coys [illegible] to be collected 12 noon on 9th & conveyed to new Camp [illegible] at [illegible] Rifle Range – [illegible] arranging authority to retain these Tentage – borrowed from Cologne [illegible] Corps.	
	9		Visited ADOS office for conference of DOS in Corps on subject of [illegible] for releasable RAOC personnel – Cross postings & promotions – I am self contained [illegible] promotions to fill establishment & have selected suitable Infantry men & Gunners (alternatively) to relieve all my storemen & clerks (RAOC). Saw [illegible] after conference & asked if he would authorise the transfer of many attached Infantry as I wanted to complete to RAOC in preference to Gunners who are not [illegible] suitable. – He will put matter before DOC for decision – [illegible] the [illegible] belong has no objection to their transfer. Returned 9 Gunners to Cologne Depot as unsuitable & surplus to my requirements.	
	10		Received instructions [illegible] a newly formed Camp at [illegible] with [illegible] (from Race course & [illegible] from Cologne Depot) Tables & forms & other miscellaneous accommodation stores by 13th [illegible]. Tables & forms [illegible] be made up locally as [illegible] cannot provide material or [illegible] work. Referred [illegible] for them to [illegible] Corps for approval & [illegible] ADOS (P) Cologne for provision at [illegible], owing to difficulty of local requisitioning.	

A7092 Wt. W12839/M1293 750,000. 1/17. D. D & L., Ltd. Forms/C2118/14.

Instructions regarding War Diaries and Intelligence Summaries are contained in F. S. Regs., Part II. and the Staff Manual respectively. Title pages will be prepared in manuscript.

WAR DIARY
or
INTELLIGENCE SUMMARY.
(Erase heading not required.)

Army Form C. 2118.

Place	Date	Hour	Summary of Events and Information	Remarks and references to Appendices
ODENTHAL	11		Visited Berg Gladbach & Mulheim & placed urgent requisitions for Tables & forms thro Area Commandants. Only small quantities obtainable by 13th in Glad Bach – Mulheim promised to produce balance if at all possible & to notify me numbers which could be collected on 13th. Reviewed the requisitions previously placed in Gladbach. 70 Fly Sprayers & 14 beds available – Meat safes & 500 yds Butter Muslin not yet available. Found 10,000 wooden washing [illegible] available in Gladbach from civilian source – requisitioned 1,000 for distribution to units & equipment of Gladbach Camp.	Table
	12.		Informed that Commandant Cologne had cancelled my requisition in Mulheim as it is in Cologne area for administrative [illegible] & that it is requisitioning area for II Corps. Instructed to apply to ADOS (P) [illegible] this has already been done – Asked ADOS II Corps to [illegible] supplies for Cologne.	
	13.		Inspected equipment of 89 Field Amb – who are [illegible] Stretchers – [illegible] attended – also Wheeler & [illegible] Very little u/s equipment for inspection – Vehicles in good condition. [illegible] Mob Table [illegible] & list of u/s & deficiencies – [illegible] Visited ADOS (P) Office & was informed that tables & forms [illegible] obtained & that SPO 275 [illegible] must be followed.	

A7092 Wt. W12839/M1293 750,000. 1/17. D. D & L., Ltd. Forms/C2118/14.

Instructions regarding War Diaries and Intelligence Summaries are contained in F. S. Regs., Part II. and the Staff Manual respectively. Title pages will be prepared in manuscript.

WAR DIARY
or
INTELLIGENCE SUMMARY.
(Erase heading not required.)

Army Form C. 2118.

Place	Date	Hour	Summary of Events and Information	Remarks and references to Appendices
ODENTHAL	14th		In view of urgency asked H.Q. II Corps to obtain authority of C.O.S. for issue of Tables & forms from Cologne Depot to this Div – 225 forms only allotted. Informed G. of action taken. Collected 22 Tables & 25 forms from German firm in Berg Gladbach as arranged by Staff Capt Civil Liaison, & delivered to Dellbrück Camp. Hastened manufacture of balance of the 150 Tables required & cancelled balance of forms.	
	15th		Requisition passed to Staff Capt. Civil Liaison, Berg Gladbach for balance of accommodation Stores under G of W Circular 74, required but not available in store for Dellbrück Camp. General Routine work.	
	16th		General Routine work.	
	17th		Notified as J–3 day, J day being date of move forward of Allies into unoccupied Territory. Returned all stores & shop equipment not required in open warfare to I.C.P. Mulheim. This renders my Detachment mobile provided all stores awaiting issue to units can be issued before moving.	
	18th		All units returned their surplus Govt stores to I.C.P. direct. Visited I.C.P. to see if they had any serviceable G.S. limber wagons & No 200 wheels available for exchange as I had previously visited I.O.M. No 10 (L) Workshops & found that he had condemned 2 limbers of the 7 sent in by M.G.B.n & also 8 of the wheels, as beyond repair. Instructed I.O.M. to ensure all vehicles belonging to units of this Div.n sent to him for repair are completed & collected by units to-day or tomorrow without fail. Found I.O.M. had been unable to repair 4. Vickers gun crossheads sent to him by M.G.B.n over a month ago. These crossheads are urgently required to put 4 guns into action. Arranged with O.O. I.C.P. to issue 2 limbered wagons & 8 wheels to M.G.B.n on application – Proceeded to Ordnance Depot Cologne-Nippes, saw O.O. re issue of the authorised reserves of Lewis & Vickers guns which I am drawing by lorry to-day	

A7092 Wt. W128/M1293 750,000. 1/17. D. D & L., Ltd. Forms/C2118/14.

Instructions regarding War Diaries and Intelligence Summaries are contained in F. S. Regs., Part II. and the Staff Manual respectively. Title pages will be prepared in manuscript.

WAR DIARY
or
INTELLIGENCE SUMMARY.
(Erase heading not required.)

Army Form C. 2118.

Place	Date	Hour	Summary of Events and Information	Remarks and references to Appendices
OBENTHAL			also borrowed 4 Tripods Mk 4 with Crosshead complete from A.I.A. at the Depot. Took them back in car & handed them over to the party of Machine Gunners drawing vehicles from I.O.M. Informed the officer i/c party that he could exchange his u/s Limbers & wheels at I.C.S. Malheim if he took them there either to day or tomorrow. He said he would send down tomorrow as his company was not moving till J day.	
	19th		Obtained 2 No 20b wheels for Trav. Kitchen for 51st Hants from u/s Travelling Kitchens at Railhead – Unit has one Kitchen immobile at present but has also[illegible] indent for one wheel only. Delivered the wheels to unit by lorry delivering new Vickers gun & other Stores to M.G. Bn. Latter Bn have 28 Wheels No 20 A on indent – which I have already hastened. Collected Tentage from Sellbrock Camp & brought to my Store instead of handing it into I.C.S. as orders received that tomorrow would not be J day & "Q" may require it for units who have moved up to perimeter if move forward is indefinitely delayed.	
	20th		Returned all accommodation Stores from Sellbrock to I.C.S. Transferred some Tentage direct to 3rd Bde at Burg. & a smaller quantity to 126 Bde RFA in Burg. Brought balance back to my Store.	
	21st		~~[illegible]~~ Collected & delivered ~~[illegible]~~ Hurricane Lamps to D.A.P.M. for traffic Control & Blankets & Ground-sheets to A & B/HAC 126 Bde for re-inforcements who arrived without any by car. General Routine work.	

Place	Date	Summary of Events & Information.
ODENTHAL	22	Overdue ~~SD clothing~~ Boots & necessaries etc received from Base. – No SD clothing for June yet received altho' Base have been hastened twice. In view of probable ~~move~~ this clothing cannot be issued to units till conditions are more settled. Arranged to deliver all stores available including some urgent deficit stores to 2nd & 3rd Bdes & Arty & wired 1st Bde to collect. There will clear stores.
"	23.	Visited 3rd Bde HQ. MG Bn, 15th Hants & 2nd Bde HQ. Staff Capts do not want ~~stores~~ SD clothing issued for present until it is decided ~~that~~ whether Div moves forward or back to old locations. MG Bn urgently requires the 28 wheels outstanding to them. Reviewed outstandings with QM 15 Hants & investigated their lack of clothing & other items of equipment due to reception of badly equipped drafts – took note of specially urgent requirements & took action on my return to stores. No undue delay this end in making units indents & all SD clothing demanded issued & present months supply awaiting issue. Found unit with only 1 suit SD per man – asked Co to put in excess demand thro' G to complete to 2 suits per man as other units in Div have 2 suits per man.
"	24	Overdue SD clothing received from Base – Considerable number of S.D. Jackets & Pantaloons deficient owing to stock at Calais having been transferred to Cologne. Re demanded these deficiencies on Special Bulk demand to be drawn on 26th from Cologne, who now function for supply of all clothing & necessaries. Section 9 stores is out of grease & soap which should have been drawn on 19th not drawn then owing to motor lorries for move – arranged to draw on 26th.

Place	Date	Summary of Events & Information.
OBENTHAL.	25th	Stores in Sections 3, 4, 7, 10b & 21 now to be demanded & drawn from Cologne in addition to clothing & Sec 9 & Anti-gas. July 4th & every fortnight after allotted the day for collection. July 3rd & every fortnight for S.D. clothing & Section 9. General Routine work.
	26th.	Delivered S.D. clothing & all other available stores to 126 Bde R.F.A., 2nd Bde units ~~[illegible]~~ as units are still standing-to & now urgently require these stores.
	27th	Delivered S.D. clothing & all other available stores to 3rd Bde units & 113 Bde R.F.A. for same reason as for stores issued yesterday. 1st Bde HQ collected large quantity of entrenching tools & picketing gear required to complete their mob equipment which had been allowed to become deficient. About 9,000 sets web equipment less Belts waist needed from Base to replace all leather equipment in use.
	28th	General Routine work. Belts waist & other components received from Base to complete total number of sets of web equipment demanded. Arranged to issue this equipment to the [illegible] Bdes in order one at a time commencing with 1st Bde. Owing to [illegible] of [illegible] to-day units will probably move back to their old locations in a few days. No more issues will be made until after the move back has been completed. Attended Conference at A.D.O.S. office & fixed up new constitution of my staff now all releasable personnel have been demobbed & replaced by Infantry men awaiting transfer to R.A.O.C. My establishment of NCOs & men now completed.

Place.	Date	Summary of Events & Information
OBENTHAL	29th	Dellbruck Musketry Camp to be started again – Arranged to withdraw all accomodation stores from ICS & re-issue to Camp – Delivered all available Tentage from my stores to this Camp – also collected some Tentage handed in to ICS & some extra tentage allotted by Corps from ICS & delivered to Camp. Further Tentage to complete required establishment to be withdrawn from 3rd Bde & 126 Bde RFA on A & B days i.e. on days when move back takes place (not yet notified)
	30th	AA & QMG approved transfer of 4 Infantry fatigue men of 52 Division to RAOC to complete my establishment of Storemen. One Employment Coy Clerk attached to be transferred to RAOC to complete my clerical establishment. Unsuitable Gunners to be returned to Cologne Ord. Depot in ICS. 3 Suitable Gunners at Railhead to be transferred to RAOC & Both RAOC NCO & man of Railhead Ordnance Staff on leave together one special & one ordinary – Arranged for one of the 3 Gunners to take charge under occasional supervision by one of my WOs & myself – These gunners have completed 21 days probation & are quite suitable for transfer. Obtained latrine buckets for Dellbruck Camp from Cologne Depot under authority from DDOS Army. Tables for Camp urgently required – Cannot obtain quickly by requisition locally & not at all from Cologne. Referred question to CRE under No 2752.

30/6/19 [illegible] Major DADOS 5th Div

SECRET

DADOS

WAR DIARY or ~~INTELLIGENCE SUMMARY.~~

(Erase heading not required.)

D.A.D.O.S. Southern Divn B.A.R.

July, 1919.

Army Form C. 2118.

Instructions regarding War Diaries and Intelligence Summaries are contained in F. S. Regs., Part II. and the Staff Manual respectively. Title pages will be prepared in manuscript.

Place	Date	Hour	Summary of Events and Information	Remarks and references to Appendices
Odenthal.	1st		Collected Tentage from 3rd Bde units at Burg - Delivered same to Dellbrück Camp to complete to scale required. Put balance into stock at my store at disposal of "G". Move back to old location completed by all units - old refitting arrangements can therefore be continued.	
"	2nd		Wrote to "G" re their refitting arrangements, after attending Decrot Conference at ADOS office - ADOS has withdrawn another W.O. from me for duty at ICS leaving only one W.O. to run my Stores & 2 RAOC men in addition. Present refitting arrangements involve all my staff being out on lorries & work at store is held up. also the proper training & supervision of attached men on probation cannot be carried out. Suggested that my store be enlarged by an annexe to be built on to it by RE & that all stores be properly laid out ready for collection by units transport (either H.T or borrowed M.T.) twice monthly.	
"	3rd		Visited SW HQ & saw AA & QMG re above & other matters - Supply of Badges Cap & Titles especially. Arranged to see ADOS Provision at GHQ Roeck & get them to hasten them from Home. Re refitting - "G" approve the addition to my store & instructs CRE to do the work. Refitting arrangements to hold for present until M T can be lent to units for collection purposes. An Employment Coy clerk to be sent to me for training & to assist in clerical work	

Instructions regarding War Diaries and Intelligence Summaries are contained in F. S. Regs., Part II. and the Staff Manual respectively. Title pages will be prepared in manuscript.

WAR DIARY
or
INTELLIGENCE SUMMARY.
(*Erase heading not required.*)

Army Form C. 2118.

Place	Date	Hour	Summary of Events and Information	Remarks and references to Appendices
Odenthal	4th		General Routine work.	
	5th		Submitted draft for D.R.O. instructing units when indenting for ordnance to demand stores of one vocab. section only on each sheet. If this is not done it will mean a lot of extra work in my office as ~~[illegible]~~ Cologne requires demands submitted thus. General Routine work.	
	6th		Published instructions to all concerned re new supply arrangements. 1st & 2nd Infty Bdes to draw from my store. Gunners to draw as before & deliver to 3rd Bde units. Div troops draw from my stores.	
	7th		General Routine work.	
	8th		New programme giving list of stores now supplied by Cologne Depot & dates allotted to formations for drawing [illegible]. All Sections except 14–21A inclusive now based on Cologne. Issued instructions to store accordingly.	
	9th		Collected & delivered kitchen utensils & chairs to [illegible] Camp. These stores were requisitioned at the end of last month.	
	10th		General Routine work.	

D. D. & L., London, E.C. (A8001) Wt. W1771/M2031 750,000 5/17 Sch. 52 Forms/C2118/14

Instructions regarding War Diaries and Intelligence Summaries are contained in F. S. Regs., Part II. and the Staff Manual respectively. Title pages will be prepared in manuscript.

WAR DIARY
or
INTELLIGENCE SUMMARY.
(Erase heading not required.)

Army Form C. 2118.

Place	Date	Hour	Summary of Events and Information	Remarks and references to Appendices
Odenthal	11th		Hastened supply of an extra 1,000 Beds folding from A.D.O.S. Provision. These are very urgently required for a Battalion sleeping on Stone floors of a factory at Berg Gladbach. 700 Beds off the original demand received & distribution given to Store.	
	12th		General Routine work. The 150 Tables requisitioned from Berg Gladbach will be available for collection at the rate of 30 per day commencing to-day. 60 are required on temporary loan by 52nd Warwicks & H.Q. Div Arty for Educational Exam. purposes. Arranged with Staff Capt Civil Duties Berg Gladbach for the loan of them on condition that these units deliver them to Dellbruck Musketry Camp when finished with.	
	13th		General Routine work.	
	14th		General Routine work.	
	15th		Collected 36 Tables from Requisition & delivered to Dellbruck Camp. The C.R.A. requires 50 Tables on loan for Div Arty Sports on 23rd inst. Arranged for them to draw 50 next Thursday 17th inst. Wrote to O.C. 52nd Devons at Dellbruck Camp asking for the total number of tables at the Camp. Unit should have collected sufficient timber from C.R.E. on 10th inst as arranged by me with G. & C.R.E. to make up 150 Tables locally in accordance with S.R.O. 2752. If they have done this – no more complete Tables will be required at the Camp & the 50 borrowed by C.R.A. will be available ~~for other~~ to meet other requirements.	

(A8001) Wt. W1771/M2031 750,000 5/17 D. D. & L. London, E.C. Sch. 52 Forms/C2118/14

Instructions regarding War Diaries and Intelligence Summaries are contained in F. S. Regs., Part II. and the Staff Manual respectively. Title pages will be prepared in manuscript.

WAR DIARY
or
INTELLIGENCE SUMMARY.
(Erase heading not required.)

Army Form C. 2118.

Place	Date	Hour	Summary of Events and Information	Remarks and references to Appendices
Odenthal	16th.		A German woman arrested by my night guard stealing leather half soles from my store which adjoins her house. A charge forwarded to A.P.M. with evidence of the guard. This charge will be investigated by a Summary British Court at Berg Gladbach on the 21st inst.	
	17th.		Visited C.O. of 51st Devons to find out his urgent requirements to complete the turnout of 500 officers & O.Rs of his Bn. who are representing the Rhine Army at the Belgian Peace Celebrations in Brussels on 21st. Caps SD - months allowance due from the 18th inst. - Also SD clothing - but an extra 50 suits required - arranged issue from surplus stock. Issued oil for making Steel Helmets shine on Service +SC Paint for same. Also flannelette for repair of Shirt Patches. Issued 1 Bipod Lewis Gun from Armourers shop to replace one lost from unit's equipment. Thus all requirements met.	
	18th.		Have reason to believe that units are not returning all U/S stores when replaced by new & that indents are submitted to replace U/S whereas in many cases the articles to be replaced have been lost & units give the wrong certificate to avoid having to explain losses & to charge individuals the value of them.	

D. D. & L., London, E.C. (A8001) Wt. W1771/M2031 750,000 5/17 Sch. 52 Forms/C2118/14

Instructions regarding War Diaries and Intelligence Summaries are contained in F. S. Regs., Part II. and the Staff Manual respectively. Title pages will be prepared in manuscript.

WAR DIARY
or
INTELLIGENCE SUMMARY.
(Erase heading not required.)

Army Form C. 2118.

Place	Date	Hour	Summary of Events and Information	Remarks and references to Appendices
Odenthal.	18th Cont.		I submitted draft for D.R.O.s instructing units to return u/s Stores at time indents for replacement were submitted. Stores such as Clothing, Boots, Harness & Saddlery, Infantry '14 & '08 equipment & Wheels which units must retain in use until replaced, are excepted from this order. If the above is not carried out the indents will not be acted upon. ~~Units were~~ Units were also instructed to give explanation for losses & to comply with S.R.O. 5521 in such cases.	
	19th		Cologne Depot now require all indents submitted in Duplicate to save work in preparing Issue Orders. Published D.R.O. instructing units to submit all detail indents in Triplicate. Bulk indents are still required in single only as all such demands are extracted to our Consolidated Demands.	
	20th		A large percentage of indents passed by me are being returned by C.O.O. Indents Cologne asking for further certificates from units in the case of losses & unserviceable Stores. These certificates are not required by any existing orders & I consider that if all regulations are observed & that I consider ~~the~~ demands are in order the C.O.O. has no authority to raise observations on them. Full investigation is made of all abnormal demands & all indents carefully checked in my office before submission to Cologne. Wrote to C.O.O. pointing out above.	

D. D. & L., London, E.C. (A5031) Wt. W1771/M2031 750,000 5/17 Sch. 52 Forms/C2118/14

Instructions regarding War Diaries and Intelligence Summaries are contained in F. S. Regs., Part II. and the Staff Manual respectively. Title pages will be prepared in manuscript.

WAR DIARY
or
INTELLIGENCE SUMMARY.
(Erase heading not required.)

Army Form C. 2118.

Place	Date	Hour	Summary of Events and Information	Remarks and references to Appendices
Odenthal	21st		most units are failing to comply with the various G.R.O.s & D.R.O.s governing preparation & submission of indents. The latter are returned to units for these orders to be complied with. General Routine work.	
	22nd		Visited 9th Gloucester Regt Pioneers & saw Adjutant & Q.M. Supply of Stores & refitting arrangements quite satisfactory. Unit wants outstanding Cap Badges hastened & Clamping Screws for Musketry Tripods which they allege were not issued to them with their allotted musketry gear to be issued as soon as possible. Arranged to hasten Cap Badges from Home thro' D.D.O.S. Provision G.H.Q. - Investigated deficiency of clamping screws. My storeman confirms correct issue but as unit have apparently lost them - I wrote to D.D.O.S.(P) to make provision for replacing them. Unit placed their stock of new & partworn S.D. clothing into the I.C.S. when ordered to be prepared to move forward on 18 ult. On applying to withdraw it again they found most of it had been stolen from the I.C.S. & accordingly they want it made up by indenting. Told them to do so ~~& I would~~ ~~myself~~ take it up with I.C.S. They should not have ~~returned~~ handed in Clothing to I.C.S. as surplus Boot Stores in the first place	

D. D. & L., London, E.C. (A8001) Wt. W1771/M2031 750,000 5/17 Sch. 52 Forms/C2118/14

Army Form C. 2118.

WAR DIARY
or
INTELLIGENCE SUMMARY.
(Erase heading not required.)

Instructions regarding War Diaries and Intelligence Summaries are contained in F. S. Regs., Part II. and the Staff Manual respectively. Title pages will be prepared in manuscript.

Place	Date	Hour	Summary of Events and Information	Remarks and references to Appendices
Odenthal	23rd		Original 8 [illegible] of War Medal Ribbon running short – will not suffice to meet all demands. Latter very difficult to estimate as conditions of award have not been received yet. ~~From newspapers~~ Conditions given in newspapers taken for checking purposes. Found several units indenting for sufficient ribbon for every off & O.R. on their ration strength – when asked to confirm all were entitled to the medal, demands were at once reduced. This being so – I return all heavy demands to units for confirmation before making issues.	
	24th		Demanded a further 10 yards of War Medal Ribbon to complete Divnl requirements. Co-opted for duty as an extra member of Divnl Tournament Demonstr. Sub Committee. Arranged to obtain all Tentage required.	
	25th		Requested approval for issue of 7 Stone Tents on temporary loan for Divnl Tournament at Kalk Sports Ground from A.A.O.S. 4 Stone Tents & 1 Marquee may also be available from my Store if other units return them promptly after use at their Sports.	
	26th		Issue of Web Equipment to units to replace Leather almost Completed. Some units very slow in drawing it & indenting for it.	

D. D. & L., London, E.C. (A8001) Wt. W1771/M2031 750,000 5/17 Sch. 52 Forms/C2118/14

Instructions regarding War Diaries and Intelligence Summaries are contained in F. S. Regs., Part II. and the Staff Manual respectively. Title pages will be prepared in manuscript.

WAR DIARY
or
INTELLIGENCE SUMMARY.
(Erase heading not required.)

Army Form C. 2118.

Place	Date	Hour	Summary of Events and Information	Remarks and references to Appendices
Odenthal	27th		Cologne Depôt not now supply Paint other than Service Colours & require to know purpose for which other Colours of Paint are are demanded. They quote a ~~G.~~ S.A.G. authority for suspension issues of which I have no trace – Asked for copy for publication in R.O.s to avoid units corresponding on this subject. General Routine work.	
	28th		Authority received to draw 7 Store tents from Cologne Depot for Army Tournament. These tents are to be handed over to Army Show representative when Tournament Show is finished. General Routine work. Attended Summary Court at Bergisch Gladbach & gave evidence as to a sack of lifts & tip pellets (leather for boot repairs) found in possession of a German civilian & being Government property.	
	29th		Collected & delivered these 7 Store tents & also collected & delivered other tentage to ~~Show~~ ground for extra personnel being sent there for constructional work. Cologne refuse to supply Steel Helmets demanded on my last Bulk indent as they are in Section 16 & are therefore supplied by Calais Base – The latter refuse to supply, stating they are in Section 1 & therefore supplied by Cologne – Submitted the correspondence to A.A.D.O.S. for a ruling as these helmets are urgently required.	

D. D. & L., London, E.C. (A8001) Wt. W1771/M2031 750,000 5/17 Sch. 52 Forms/C2118/14

Instructions regarding War Diaries and Intelligence Summaries are contained in F. S. Regs., Part II. and the Staff Manual respectively. Title pages will be prepared in manuscript.

WAR DIARY
or
INTELLIGENCE SUMMARY.
(Erase heading not required.)

Army Form C. 2118.

Place	Date	Hour	Summary of Events and Information	Remarks and references to Appendices
Odenthal.	30th		Received letter from A.D.O.S. II Corps instructing me to find a suitable site, if possible in my Divnl area for an I.C.S. in view of probable reductions in Garrison in other Corps. Bergisch Gladbach would be most suitable location but all large buildings there are fully occupied by our Divnl troops at present. Burscheid would be more central for units as at present located but suitable accommodation might be difficult to find there. Asked 'G' for their views as I do not know future movements of Divn.	
"	31st		500 yds wire gauze obtained off my Requisition order ~~[illegible]~~ submitted over two months ago. Urgently required by Artillery units especially. Passed distribution to Stores both for wire gauze demands & muslin demands - latter not obtainable wire gauze to be issued in lieu. 'G' reported complaints from units that a certain type of Class 'A' Boot issued to Infantry were far too heavy owing to the heavy steel plates fitted all over the heel & sole of a number of pairs of Boots [illegible] previously. Arranged to investigate & report numbers & dates [illegible] of these particular boots.	

W. W. Weaver [illegible]
Major
D.A.D.O.S.
[illegible] Div.

SECRET

Instructions regarding War Diaries and Intelligence Summaries are contained in F. S. Regs., Part II. and the Staff Manual respectively. Title pages will be prepared in manuscript.

August 1919

WAR DIARY ~~or INTELLIGENCE SUMMARY.~~

(Erase heading not required.)

~~D.A.D.O.S.~~ Southern Div.
B.A.R.

Army Form C. 2118.

Place	Date	Hour	Summary of Events and Information	Remarks and references to Appendices
Odenthal, Germany	1st		Pay & Mess account book taken into use. Difficulty arose over the large number of sheets required for my Detachment owing to it consisting of men of a number of different Corps & Regiments. Hastened supply of extra supply of these A.F.s & wrote to Command Paymaster asking whether ~~[illegible]~~ men attached to me could not be paid by the Units to which they belong on Casual Payment Forms to save exclusive work & delay in my office.	
	2nd		Over 1000 Beds available at O.O. 9th Corps Troops – Arranged to take 820 of these to complete Div's requirements & cancelled all outstandings on A.D.O.S. Provision S.H.Q. 500 also available with O.O. 9th Corps troops – wired – not required – in view of surplus with II Corps troops.	
	3rd		General Routine work.	
	4th		Paint Service Colour urgently required by 53rd Warwicks for Horse Show purposes. Not received from Cologne Depot off my last demand. Wired O.O. 9th Corps troops if they had any surplus – also [illegible] required by [illegible] Train for decorations on Show Ground.	
	[illegible]		Collected 7 Stove [illegible] from Cologne Depot on Cheq. Army authority & delivered to Div. Show Ground – 4 more will be available for my stock when returned from other Sports meetings.	
	5th		10M No 70 O.M.W. Light [illegible] wired in reply to numerous wires from me that 4 Cross heads for Mk IV Tripods sent to him for repair over 2 months ago have been repaired & could be collected. These are to be returned to Ordnance Depot, Nippes.	

D. D. & L., London, E.C.
(A8004) Wt. W1771/M2031 750,000 5/17 Sch. 52 Forms/C2118/14

Instructions regarding War Diaries and Intelligence Summaries are contained in F. S. Regs., Part II. and the Staff Manual respectively. Title pages will be prepared in manuscript.

WAR DIARY
or
~~INTELLIGENCE SUMMARY.~~
(Erase heading not required.)

Army Form C. 2118.

Place	Date	Hour	Summary of Events and Information	Remarks and references to Appendices
Odenthal Germany	6th		Hastened supply of Latrine Buckets (20) for Cologne Depot – demanded on loan for Div[n] Show ground. Collected Div[l] allotment of Target Material from Corps "G" & distributed according to instructions from 5th Div[n] "G". Collected & issued Latrine Buckets & Camp Kettles for [illegible] Cotton Rags to Div[n] Show ground & issued Coloured bunting for flags to O.C. [illegible] for Decorations at Show ground.	
	7th		Authority given for requisition of Camp Combs & issue on scale laid down in S.R. Pt II – is 1 per 3 animals – Found out by lorry that O.O. 9th Corps troops had large quantity surplus. Asked if I could collect 600. Balance of Tentage required at Div[l] Show ground issued.	
	8th		O.O. 9 C.T. replied that ~~them~~ any number up to 2000 Combs could be collected & arranged to collect by car first opportunity. Div[l] Horse Show & Sports held to-day. Sent 50% of my staff to the show by lorry & closed down Stores & shops as far as possible.	
	9th		2/4 Hants, being inspected shortly by Army Council requiring the S.D. clothing demanded last week & due for issue next Thursday – This demand includes ration plus excess demand. Wired Ordnance Depot Cologne asking if this clothing could be specially issued in time for this inspection – Replied "Yes".	

D. D. & L., London, E.C. (A5071) Wt. W1771/M2031 750,000 5/17 Sch. 52 Forms/C2118/14

Instructions regarding War Diaries and Intelligence Summaries are contained in F. S. Regs., Part II. and the Staff Manual respectively. Title pages will be prepared in manuscript.

WAR DIARY
or
~~INTELLIGENCE~~ ~~SUMMARY~~.

(*Erase heading not required.*)

Army Form C. 2118.

Place	Date	Hour	Summary of Events and Information	Remarks and references to Appendices
Odenthal Germany	10th		Returned 55 C.I. Tents & 20 Marquees from Horse Show Ground to 00 Corps Troops. Handed over 7 Marquees to Camp Commandant of ground for Army Horse show – Collect balance of ~~Store~~ Tents & put into Store. Latrine Buckets & all Camp Kettles less 2 lost returned to Cologne Depot from Horse Show Ground.	
	11th		~~The~~ Collect 30 sets Tent Bottoms from Cologne Depot for issue to 3rd Infantry Bde. under authority of A.D.O.S.	
	12th		These tent bottoms are a double issue and are not required in addition to those already issued to 3rd Bde – Issued them to a Bn of 2nd Bde to complete an outstanding demand approved by A.D.O.S. Saw D.A.Q.M.G. [illegible] in conjunction with A.D.O.S. 4 Corps re. issue of instructions to units to demand to complete [illegible] (except equipment) & cancellation of [illegible] indents to proceed [illegible]	
	13th		Attended F.G.C.M. as prosecutor in case of Pte [illegible] attached to us as storeman who is charged with theft of stores from my stores. Cancelled all outstanding detail indents on Calais & Cologne Depots in accordance with instructions from D.O.S. to cancel outstandings as far as possible – only stores essential to comfort of troops or repair & preservation of equipment will be issued by Base in future in view of early departure of formations of Rhine Army for England. Have been [illegible] notifying cancellation & [illegible] to companies.	

B. D. & L., London, E.C. (A8004) Wt. W1771/M2031 750,000 5/17 Sch. 52 Forms/C2.118/14

WAR DIARY
or
~~INTELLIGENCE~~ ~~SUMMARY.~~
(Erase heading not required.)

Army Form C. 2118.

Instructions regarding War Diaries and Intelligence Summaries are contained in F. S. Regs., Part II. and the Staff Manual respectively. Title pages will be prepared in manuscript.

Place	Date	Hour	Summary of Events and Information	Remarks and references to Appendices
Odenthal. Germany	13th	(Cont)	as agreed at conference with D.D.O.S. This action will make the supply of Ordnance situation clear.	
	14th		General Routine work. The instructing units to demand to S.1058 not yet published – 'G' now say publication held up pending approval by G.O.C.	
	15th		Instead of despatching unserviceable Stores to Cologne Depot or any Rly via Railhead, instruction received from D.O.S. to obtain sanction of C.O.O. Cologne before despatching any more Stores to Cologne – my Returned Stores Dump will become emptied owing to this ruling as lorries now full – wired C.O.O. Cologne asking if one truck load could be returned at once.	
	16th		Collected 220 [illegible] from O.C. II Corps Troops & delivered to [illegible] Signal Coy for paper factory at Berg. Instructed 53 warrants(?) to collect books(?). General Routine work. [illegible] from [illegible] Depot.	
	17th		'G' have now issued G.R.O. instructing units to indent to complete S.1058 stating in indents which stores are & which are not required to be drawn – Visited O.O. Field Indents at C.O.O.'s Office Cologne & in view of his instructions to pass indents for essential stores only arranged with him to pass to him only indents endorsed by unit as "required to be drawn" & to file all others in my Office for record purposes only.	

D. D. & L., London, E.C. A6091 Wt. W1771/M2031 750,000 5/17 Sch. 52 Forms/C2118/14

Instructions regarding War Diaries and Intelligence Summaries are contained in F. S. Regs., Part II. and the Staff Manual respectively. Title pages will be prepared in manuscript.

WAR DIARY
or
~~INTELLIGENCE~~ ~~SUMMARY~~.
(*Erase heading not required.*)

Army Form C. 2118.

Place	Date	Hour	Summary of Events and Information	Remarks and references to Appendices
Odenthal Germany	18th		Received instructions to return all u/s stores on hand to Calais Base instead of to Cologne. This is unusual as since 15th June all ~~return~~ u/s & surplus stores have had to be sent to Cologne — Despatched 2 truck loads accordingly.	
	19th		Report unsatisfactory position of supply of Indian Clothing for Indian personnel of V.A.C. — altho repeatedly re-demanded none has been received from Base for 2 months. Gave particulars of quantities & dates of demand & asked for immediate hastening action.	
	20th		3 Store Tents issued to C.R.E. for new Training Camp. The remaining one ~~was~~ unserviceable & has be sent to Calais — leaving nil in store available for re-issue.	
	21st		H.Q. Hvy Arty reported they have returned 50 requisitioned tables lent to them for special purpose last month to the firm in Berg Gladbach who supplied them. This is entirely irregular as I have repeatedly warned the Staff Capt of Hvy Arty to return them to me for re-issue to A.E.O. for Educational purposes. In any case they should have been returned to the Burgomaster & a receipt in duplicate obtained for final settlement. Took up the matter with Hvy Arty for rectification. General Routine work.	

D. D. & L., London, E.C.
(A8004) Wt. W1771/M2031 750,000 5/17 Sch. 52 Forms/C2118/14

Instructions regarding War Diaries and Intelligence Summaries are contained in F. S. Regs., Part II. and the Staff Manual respectively. Title pages will be prepared in manuscript.

WAR DIARY
or
~~INTELLIGENCE SUMMARY.~~
(Erase heading not required.)

Army Form C. 2118.

Place	Date	Hour	Summary of Events and Information	Remarks and references to Appendices
Ohlinthal. Germany.	22nd		one Soyers Stove 4 Funnels cleaning chamber & 7lbs washing Soda & 4 ladles for pouring hot soda water into funnels urgently required by 3rd Bde for refitting [illegible] in their area – Arranged issue of Stove from stock of [illegible] for purpose of washing goods & [illegible] Gave orders for funnels to be made up in [illegible] & [illegible] wired that ladles were not available or procurable for the purpose. General Routine work.	
	23rd		9th Glosters (Pioneers) report present refilling arrangements are unsatisfactory owing to uncertainty of time of arrival of my refilling lorry at 3rd Bde supply dumps (Found fault lies as much with units transport as with my lorry) & insufficiency of time for proper checking – Unit asked if they could draw from my store once a week. Informed them this would be much more convenient to me & that I agreed. Instructed Store accordingly & Routine work	
	24th		General Routine work. Visited COO Cologne & discussed matters concerning issues off indents submitted by us – Asked if he could let me know where I could draw furniture at reasonable rates.	
	25th		Wired COO Cologne for his [illegible] instruction for another truck load of u/s Stores – COO replied referring me to instruction just sent out by him to all formations – giving programme for return of all Stores handed in by troops to Cologne depot – This further received this A.D.O.S. – issued instructions to Store accordingly.	

D. D. & L., London, E.C. (A8001) Wt. W1771/M2031 750,000 5/17 Sch. 52 Forms/C2118/14

Instructions regarding War Diaries and Intelligence Summaries are contained in F. S. Regs., Part II. and the Staff Manual respectively. Title pages will be prepared in manuscript.

WAR DIARY
or
~~INTELLIGENCE SUMMARY.~~
(Erase heading not required.)

Army Form C. 2118.

Place	Date	Hour	Summary of Events and Information	Remarks and references to Appendices
Odenthal. Germany	26th		Reviewed Tentage records & stock – disposed of all incomplete tentage to Cologne Depot – checked all issues & receipts & took stock, all discrepancies cleared up. Informed G of this – I have a surplus of C.S.L Tents to make up any deficiencies shewn by units returns.	
	27th		Instructions received from G to draw 3 Store tents from Cologne Depot & issue to A/113 Bde R.F.A as I have no stock available. Visited the A.D.O.S Provision office Cologne & asked the Requisitioning Officer if he could inform me if [illegible] could hire wicker & club chairs for Divl. Rest Station. He promised to find out if any such furniture rendered surplus by units [illegible] could be obtained as it was impossible to hire any in Cologne.	
	28th		Instructions from D.A.G regarding disposal of stores to be handed in by units & formations moving to the U.K. have been received almost daily [illegible] last 3 weeks. G have taken no action as they get [illegible] to continual [illegible]. [illegible] A.D.O.S II Corps inspected my store & advised me to get in all surplus stores & vehicles as early as possible & dispose of them in accordance with instructions from D.O.S II Corps Cologne	

Army Form C. 2118.

WAR DIARY
or
INTELLIGENCE ~~SUMMARY~~.

(*Erase heading not required.*)

Instructions regarding War Diaries and Intelligence Summaries are contained in F. S. Regs., Part II. and the Staff Manual respectively. Title pages will be prepared in manuscript.

Place	Date	Hour	Summary of Events and Information	Remarks and references to Appendices
Odenthal Germany	28th	(Cont)	my own store almost clear. – Surplus requisitioned rugs & plates & bed- are being handed over at once to the Burgomaster & arrangements have been made to dispose of the large quantities of unserviceable & surplus stores now coming in from units – a programme for loading & despatch of trucks to Base sent to my representative at Railhead & to O.C. Cologne Group & O.O. [illegible]. A new depot to be known as Base Reception Depot opening at Cologne for receipt of most surplus & R.S. stores.	
	29th		Wrote to [illegible] pointing out advantages of getting in all surplus [illegible] S1058 at once – this will avoid congestion at the moment & the heavy labour of ordnance personnel to clear up – The Light Div has found 50 surplus vehicles in their Div. Asked G to instruct units to report all surpluses to me for disposal forthwith & then to certify they hold no surplus transport. Submitted 2 drafts to the D.A.G. on above subject.	
	30th		These 2 drafts put before by the G. Large batches of certificates of completeness [illegible] were received from several units – returned most of them for completion & amendment to put them in order before filing them in my office.	
	31st		Have asked for the dispersal of my Sergeant at Railhead who is a [illegible] & arranged for his relief from among my own detachment.	

W M Weare
Major
D.A.D.O.S.
8th Div.

D. D. & L., London, E.C. (A8004) Wt. W1771/M2031 750,000 5/17 Sch. 52 Forms/C2118/14

SECRET SEPTEMBER 1919. **WAR DIARY** ~~or INTELLIGENCE SUMMARY.~~ D.A.D.O.S. Southern. Divn. Army Form C. 2118.

Instructions regarding War Diaries and Intelligence Summaries are contained in F. S. Regs., Part II. and the Staff Manual respectively. Title pages will be prepared in manuscript.

(*Erase heading not required.*)

Place	Date	Hour	Summary of Events and Information	Remarks and references to Appendices
Ottenbach Germany	1/9/19.		Closed my Retail Store & incorporated it with Bulk Stores to economise in personnel - shortage due to heavy leave allotment. Moved Armourers, Tailors & Shoemakers into old Retail Store - this leaves the hall previously occupied by shops vacant & available to accommodate a larger receipt of U/S & surplus stores from units.	
"	2/9/19		General Routine work.	
"	3/9/19		Received collected précis of instructions regarding dispatch of units to UK from G.; also detailed instructions from A.D.O.S. II Corps regarding ~~the~~ record & returns of stores which can now be returned by units of formations who will proceed home shortly, & of stores which will be returned after the departure of units. Asked G. if they would publish instructions for submission of lists on ~~[illegible]~~ pro-forma prepared by A.D.O.S. G. instructed me to take no further action for present - only surpluses G.1098 are to be returned at once & instructions to this effect have already been issued - Equipment of M.G. & T.M. Bs already returned to O.C.S. Kitbags with units is still required - All U/S stores should have been returned by units when demanding to complete G.1098 - no further instructions considered necessary.	

D. D. & L., London, E.C. (A8001) Wt. W1771/M2031 750,000 5/17 Sch. 52 Forms/C2118/14

Army Form C. 2118.

WAR DIARY
or
INTELLIGENCE SUMMARY.
(Erase heading not required.)

Instructions regarding War Diaries and Intelligence Summaries are contained in F. S. Regs., Part II. and the Staff Manual respectively. Title pages will be prepared in manuscript.

Place	Date	Hour	Summary of Events and Information	Remarks and references to Appendices
Odenthal – Germany	4/9/19		400 Blankets urgently required for 2 Coys of a Bn billeted under canvas at Bellincourt Musketry Camp. – The Bn returned their 2nd Blanket per man when in billets. As units are still allowed to retain 2 per man this demand passed – none available for immediate issue at Ies. Demanded on Calais & marked Urgent. Issue could be made from large stocks of washed & disinfected blankets returned there 3 months ago (if not already disposed of)	
"	5/9/19		Instructions received from G that no war equipment of units was to be returned as laid down in previous instructions. Another letter received from H.Q. stating that all formations in 2nd Corps would not move to U.K. as arranged – No further arrangements or instructions for return of stores, therefore necessary but units should be urged to clear out all surpluses. Several surpluses in transport already reported – Instructed units to send these by road to Neuss on Tuesdays & Fridays when total surpluses in Bn are known & after allowing any to replace deficiencies. Visited AAQMG II Corps & DADOS Brigade 9th	
"	6/9/19		My leave to U.K. approved – Capt Hewson arrived to act for me while on leave.	

Instructions regarding War Diaries and Intelligence Summaries are contained in F. S. Regs., Part II. and the Staff Manual respectively. Title pages will be prepared in manuscript.

WAR DIARY
or
INTELLIGENCE SUMMARY.

(Erase heading not required.)

Army Form C. 2118.

Place	Date	Hour	Summary of Events and Information	Remarks and references to Appendices
Odenthal Germany	7/9/19		General Routine work – Handed over to Capt K.M. Hewson RAVC Reported his arrival to DDVS DVS & ADVS & informed DAAG 5th Div & Camp Commandant of date of taking over. Major Bearman Proceeded on leave to UK – 8th – 22nd inclusive	
"	8/9/19		General Routine Work – ADVS asked to arrange disposal of German vehicles held in the Division	
"	9/9/19 to 16/9/19		General Routine	

D. D. & L., London, E.C.
(A8004) Wt. W1771/M2031 750,000 5/17 Sch. 52 Forms/C2118/14

Army Form C. 2118.

Instructions regarding War Diaries and Intelligence Summaries are contained in F. S. Regs., Part II. and the Staff Manual respectively. Title pages will be prepared in manuscript.

WAR DIARY
or
INTELLIGENCE SUMMARY.
(*Erase heading not required.*)

Place	Date	Hour	Summary of Events and Information	Remarks and references to Appendices
Odenthal Germany	17.		Lt H. A. Elliot arrived to relieve Capt Hewson, who was under orders to proceed to Berlin	
	18		Lt Elliott took over from Capt. Hewson.	
"	19		General Routine Work	
"	20		"	
"	21		"	
"	22		"	

D. D. & L., London, E.C. (A8001) Wt. W1771/M2031 750,000 5/17 Sch. 52 Forms/C2118/14

Instructions regarding War Diaries and Intelligence Summaries are contained in F. S. Regs., Part II. and the Staff Manual respectively. Title pages will be prepared in manuscript.

WAR DIARY
or
INTELLIGENCE SUMMARY.
(Erase heading not required.)

Army Form C. 2118.

Place	Date	Hour	Summary of Events and Information	Remarks and references to Appendices
Odenthal, Germany	23		Major A.M.E. BEAVAN returned from leave & resumed duties of DADOS.	
	24		General Routine work. My demobilisation approved by DOS & a relief arranged Lt Col. Kirkby. ADOS 4th Corps will take over from me when he has cleared up his present duties i.e. in about a months time. To enable me to be demobbed about 1st Oct as I have requested, ADOS II Corps arranges for Lieut. Elliot RGA to act as DADOS between my departure & the arrival of Lt Col Kirkby. Submitted these arrangements to A.A. & Q.M.G. 5th Div for approval.	
	25.		Sent Lt Elliot to inspect Harness & Saddlery of 113 Bde R.F.A. who have complained that it is in a very bad state & wish to have it replaced by new. Saw A.A. & Q.M.G. - he approves these arrangements & will arrange for my papers to be prepared & an allotment for dispersal given me on Oct 1st. Instructions received from ADOS II Corps to evacuate surplus vehicles to Gen No 10 OMW Light instead of sending them to Cologne - latter Depot will not accept direct.	
	26.		Wired all units who reported having surplus vehicles to send all British vehicles to No 10. OMW. & all German vehicles to II Corps ADO & Abandoned Stores Dump, Leverkusen. Copies of all receipts obtained to be sent to the office by units. Report on condition of H.S. of 113 Bde RFA sent to A.D.M.G. - Sets good on the whole but certain parts are bad & require replacement.	

D. D. & L., London, E.C. (A8001) Wt. W1771/M2031 750,000 5/17 Sch. 52 Forms/C2118/14

Instructions regarding War Diaries and Intelligence Summaries are contained in F. S. Regs., Part II. and the Staff Manual respectively. Title pages will be prepared in manuscript.

WAR DIARY
or
INTELLIGENCE SUMMARY.
(Erase heading not required.)

Army Form C. 2118.

Place	Date	Hour	Summary of Events and Information	Remarks and references to Appendices
Odenthal, Germany.	27		All Tentage to be withdrawn from units – as troops have been ordered into billets & huts. Wrote letter published instructing all units to return Tentage to any store alongside & report totals returned to C.O. Officer. This Tentage can be sent to Cologne Depot by rail in accordance with existing programmes. Instructed W.O. i/c store accordingly & warned him not to accept wet Tentage.	
	28.		ADOS II Corps visited store & inspected store shops & receipt dumps & gave permission for Tentage to be sent direct to Cologne by M.E. in spite of instructions received from Cologne Depot thro' ADOS to the effect that Tentage must be sent to I.C.S. & evacuated from there to Cologne. Cologne Depot have accepted 2 consignments of Tents previously direct so I do not anticipate any objection now – This arrangement of sending direct will save double handling at I.C.S.	
	29.		General Routine work. ADOS II Corps requires a return showing all Releasable & Retainable W.O.s N.C.O.s & men giving reasons why releasable or retainable as case may be. He requires the particulars carefully checked by officer & all documents scrutinized, & if any doubt exists as to any man being voluntarily enlisted or conscripted, information to be obtained from O i/c Records.	

D. D. & L., London, E.C. (A8001) Wt. W1771/M2031 750,000 5/17 Sch. 52 Forms/C2118/14

Instructions regarding War Diaries and Intelligence Summaries are contained in F. S. Regs., Part II. and the Staff Manual respectively. Title pages will be prepared in manuscript.

WAR DIARY
or
INTELLIGENCE SUMMARY.
(Erase heading not required.)

Place	Date	Hour	Summary of Events and Information	Remarks and references to Appendices
Odenthal	30th		General Routine work. ~~All~~ demobilisation & leave held up on account of Railway Strike in U.K. Lt. Col Hinkley, ~~A.D.O.S~~ 4th Corps visited me. Gave him details of procedure in various points in this Dept & the most important questions at present outstanding. He expects to take over from me on 10th inst & to introduce himself to Gen'l 'Q' to-day.	
			W. S. Swan Major, D.A.D.O.S. Southern Divn	

D. D. & L., London, E.C. (A8001) Wt. W1771/M2031 750,000 5/17 Sch. 52 Forms/C2118/14

D. A. D. O. S.

October

WAR DIARY
or
INTELLIGENCE SUMMARY.
(*Erase heading not required.*)

Confidential

Army Form C. 2118.

Instructions regarding War Diaries and Intelligence Summaries are contained in F. S. Regs., Part II. and the Staff Manual respectively. Title pages will be prepared in manuscript.

Place	Date	Hour	Summary of Events and Information	Remarks and references to Appendices
Odenthal	Oct 1st		Moved my clerks office into rooms in the village vacated by Armourer's Shop. Retained my own office in the Schloss & asked Signals to arrange ~~[illegible]~~ alteration in telephone system to suit this arrangement. P.V.R. Book completed — Total rations & cash balance correct. Arranged with Staff Capt. 3rd Bde to maintain 3rd Bde Ordnance refilling at the same place as before i.e. at the late Supply refilling point in WERMELSKIRCHEN at same time, & on same day as Supply refilling point. 2nd & 3rd Bde are now together at Burscheid. ~~[illegible]~~ Sent lorry to collect Salvage from 51st Bgde. R.F.A. 2 Bde who are at Burg & too far away to refilling point — Salvage working [illegible] so could not remove it.	
	2nd		On instructions from G sent lorries to collect Salvage from R.F.A. of 3rd Bde who are too far away to return it direct. — Instructions received from G to take over all Salvage & Ordnance Stores at [illegible] Camp from the Bn now in occupation. This Bn is moving [illegible] on 4th inst. To avoid bringing this large quantity of Stores etc to my Stores not held by A.D.O.S. of Stores other than Reinforcement Stores at the Camp asked that could be all handed over to [illegible] to enable it to get away quickly — If programme for sending to Cologne	

(A8001) Wt. W1771/M2031 750,000 5/17 Sch. 52 Forms/C2118/14
D. D. & L., London, E.C.

WAR DIARY
or
INTELLIGENCE SUMMARY.
(Erase heading not required.)

Instructions regarding War Diaries and Intelligence Summaries are contained in F. S. Regs., Part II. and the Staff Manual respectively. Title pages will be prepared in manuscript.

Army Form C. 2118.

Place	Date	Hour	Summary of Events and Information	Remarks and references to Appendices
Odenthal	2nd	(Cont)	is adopted considerable delay would occur.	
	3rd		General Routine work.	
	4th		Sent Lt Elliott to inspect ordnance stores & Tentage at Dellbrück Camp & to obtain a complete list of same — also to call on Burgomeister of Berg Gladbach & inform him that we should return Requd stores to him from Dellbrück on Monday next. List obtained & on comparison with my record of issues to camp showed several additions of stores obtained by Requisition & brought there by units from time to time — ~~other~~ 17 C&L Tents more than were issued by us also appeared on list. Arranged to remove all ordnance stores both issued from store & Requisitioned on Monday 6th inst. Informed 1st Bde HQ and asked them to detail a loading party & guard under an officer to strike camp & hand over to my representative. Asked 'Q' for 3 extra lorries to report to the Camp at 9 am on 6th & can send 3 of my lorries as well.	
	5th		General Routine work.	
	6th		Sent Lt Elliott & 2 storemen to Dellbrück Camp at 9 am to check & remove all stores — Requd stores sent to Burgomeister Berg Gladbach & Tentage & other ordnance stores to [illegible] — which A.D.O.S. approved.	

D. D. & L., London, E.C. (A8004) Wt. W1771/M2031 750,000 5/17 Sch. 52 Forms/C2.118/14.

Instructions regarding War Diaries and Intelligence Summaries are contained in F. S. Regs., Part II. and the Staff Manual respectively. Title pages will be prepared in manuscript.

WAR DIARY
or
INTELLIGENCE SUMMARY.
(Erase heading not required.)

Army Form C. 2118.

Place	Date	Hour	Summary of Events and Information	Remarks and references to Appendices
Odenthal	7th		Completed removal & disposal of balance of stores from Bellbrück. Receipts given & obtained do not agree in every case.	
	8th		Sent Lt Elliott to recheck stores returned to Burgomeister & to DCS & to adjust receipts where incorrect – Clear receipt on DCS obtained & lists adjusted. My demobilisation arranged for 12th 15 when Bologna Express recommences running.	
	9th		Sent up-to-date Surplus Return to C, including those withdrawn from Bellbrück. Appropriated certain serviceable stores from those returned to me by units surplus to G1098 to meet outstanding demands of other units to complete to G1098 – Balance carefully checked, labelled & despatched to Cologne by rail thro' RDO.	
	10th		GRO published authorising issue of vests & drawers, woollen to troops & also of frost caps, cap & comforters – Gave instructions for Bath demands to be submitted on 15th inst from units demanding half the drawers demanded & an additional 2/3rds of vests demanded to be issued direct to Bath. Obtain on receipt. Received demob. allotment for all my demobilisable personnel viz 1 Sergt clerk & store clerk. This will place me in a difficult position as regards office staff as my chief clerk & one other are still on leave.	

(A8004) Wt. W1771/M2031 750,000 5/17 Sch. 52 Forms/C2118/14 D. D. & L., London, E.C.

Instructions regarding War Diaries and Intelligence Summaries are contained in F. S. Regs., Part II. and the Staff Manual respectively. Title pages will be prepared in manuscript.

WAR DIARY
or
INTELLIGENCE SUMMARY.
(*Erase heading not required.*)

Army Form C. 2118.

Place	Date	Hour	Summary of Events and Information	Remarks and references to Appendices
	10th Cont.		Wrote ~~A.A.O.~~ of 2nd Corps asking if he could let me have a Sergt Clerk at once to relieve the situation – Letter received from A.A.O. giving personnel situation in each ordnance formation of 2nd Corps & instructing D.C.S to ~~transfe~~ return one of my W.O.s to me at once. This W.O. has been urgently required for some time past to take charge of Receipt Stores. Handed over my duties to Lt Elliott on instructions from Lwr "A" Branch & reported having done so to Lwr A & A.A.O. 2nd Corps. Arranged to give Lt Elliott any information & advice he may need until I leave for demob on 13th (not 12th as previously arranged).	

[illegible] Major
A.A.O.
Southern [illegible]

Instructions regarding War Diaries and Intelligence Summaries are contained in F. S. Regs., Part II. and the Staff Manual respectively. Title pages will be prepared in manuscript.

Confidential

WAR DIARY or INTELLIGENCE SUMMARY.

(Erase heading not required.)

Army Form C. 2118.

D. A. D. O. S
Southern Division

Place	Date	Hour	Summary of Events and Information	Remarks and references to Appendices
Udental	Oct 11th		Assumed duties of D.A.D.O.S. Southern Div. Notified A.D.O.S. initial requirements of winter underwear, estimated on present strength of Division.	
"	12		General Routine	
"	13		Major Beavan left on the leave train from Cologne at 15.16 hrs. I visited C.O.O. & Stationery Depot to make an application for a typewriter, as the one previously in use was Major ~~Towns~~ Beavan's property.	
"	14		Sgt Goldsworthy (clerk) together with L/Cpl Lownds & Pte Mackenzie (Storemen) left for the Dispersal Station. In view of wire from "G" calling for ~~names~~ number of men eligible for Demobilization as per A.O. 55, I ordered a general Parade, & discovered a man, who was in possession of a letter offering him immediate employment, which had been recommended by the Advisory Committee (Ministry of Labour) in Jan. 19. He is a Shoemaker attached to the R.A.O.C. I therefore reported the matter & sent the letter to Southern Div "A"	
"	15.		Pte Brownrigg attached as clerk, who had applied for special leave owing to his young son having to undergo an operation, went	

D. D. & L., London, E.C. (A8001) Wt. W1771/M2031 750,000 5/17 Sch. 52 Forms/C2.118/14

Army Form C. 2118. 2

WAR DIARY
or
INTELLIGENCE SUMMARY.
(Erase heading not required.)

DADOS
Southern Div

Instructions regarding War Diaries and Intelligence Summaries are contained in F. S. Regs., Part II. and the Staff Manual respectively. Title pages will be prepared in manuscript.

Place	Date	Hour	Summary of Events and Information	Remarks and references to Appendices
Ovental	15		on 14 days furlough to the U.K. This much handicapped me as there was no one left who was familiar with the office work. I had therefore to ~~obtain~~ place T/Condr Kinsella (Storeman) in the office, whose assistance was essential & of much value	
"	15		I visited Division "Q" to obtain their consent that Units should be instructed to draw the 1st issue of Underclothing direct from the Baths Officer. "Q" agreed & would take up the matter with Baths Officer. Visited Baths Officer, who agreed to take all the Winter Underclothing direct from me in Bulk, as this is the only method whereby the return of the cotton drawers is ensured & it also ensures that all the men come to the baths, which has not been done	
"	16		S/Condr Wilson reported for duty from I.C.S. to whom he had been left. I was still short of 2 W.O's – one of whom was on leave, the other at the I.C.S.	
"	16		Informed by "Q" that after conferring with Baths Officer, it was decided to issue Underclothing as per G.R.O.	

D. D. & L., London, E.C.
(A8004) Wt. W1771/M2031 750,000 5/17 Sch. 52 Forms/C2118/14

3

Army Form C. 2118.

Instructions regarding War Diaries and Intelligence Summaries are contained in F. S. Regs., Part II. and the Staff Manual respectively. Title pages will be prepared in manuscript.

WAR DIARY
or
INTELLIGENCE SUMMARY.
(Erase heading not required.)

DADOS
Southern Div.

Place	Date	Hour	Summary of Events and Information	Remarks and references to Appendices
Odenthal	16		Had my office moved into a room leading into that occupied by my clerks, as having an office at the Schloss, half a mile away, was too inconvenient & impracticable. The clerks office, which used to be at the Schloss, had been moved into the village opposite the Bulk Store previously on my suggestion. On my first arrival I found the place ill-suited for a Divisional Ordnance Depot, as (a) the accommodation was poor, in consequence of which unserviceable stores had to be placed in an outhouse with no door and also in the open outside. (b) There is no public conveyance between here and Berg Gladbach, where many of the Units are quartered & Railhead is located. (c) Being deprived of the use of the car allotted to a DADOS, I ~~was~~ am unable to visit units at short notice & as often as desired, whereas had Berg Gladbach been chosen, it would be easy to visit the Units there & in the vicinity, also Divisional Hdqrs even without a car. If we stay here much longer, I propose therefore to strongly recommend that the Depot be moved to Berg Gladbach.	
"	17		Orders had been received that Valuable Stores were to be	

D. D. & L., London, E.C. (A8001) Wt. W1771/M2031 750,000 5/17 Sch. 52 Forms/C2118/14

Instructions regarding War Diaries and Intelligence Summaries are contained in F. S. Regs., Part II. and the Staff Manual respectively. Title pages will be prepared in manuscript.

WAR DIARY
or
INTELLIGENCE SUMMARY.
(Erase heading not required.)

D.A.D.O.S.
Southern Div

Army Form C. 2118.

Place	Date	Hour	Summary of Events and Information	Remarks and references to Appendices
Wental	17		returned. I arranged to collect the Valuable Stores from 126 Bdge & sent a lorry to Berg ~~B~~ Gladbach for this purpose. I personally travelled on one of the lorries & inspected the requisitioned stores at the batteries in the 126 Bdge. I found that the order that "Stores received from the Ordnance were to be returned to the Ordnance" had been too literally interpreted by some Units, as they quoted this order when asked why they did not intend to return the German beds etc to the Burgomeister and added "these stores were received from you".	
	17		Through Divisional Hdqrs Train I obtained the loan of a car & visited the 9th Gloucester at Leichlingen to inspect requisitioned goods. Received appendix Y from Q. and arranged to collect valuable stores and send them direct to the I.O.S. Sent off Pay & Mess Account also various returns, which entailed much office work being still without a Clerk.	

D. D. & L., London, E.C.
(A8004) Wt. W1771/M2031 750,000 5/17 Sch. 52 Forms/C2118/14

Instructions regarding War Diaries and Intelligence Summaries are contained in F. S. Regs., Part II. and the Staff Manual respectively. Title pages will be prepared in manuscript.

WAR DIARY
or
INTELLIGENCE SUMMARY.
(Erase heading not required.)

DADOS Southern Div.

Army Form C. 2118.

Place	Date	Hour	Summary of Events and Information	Remarks and references to Appendices
Bental	Oct 18		Paraded night-guard & instructed them in their duties, as no written orders had been handed them. I ordered one sentry to remain at the Surplus Dump, while the other patrolled around. L/Cpl Dedman deferred his demobilization for three months at the last moment. It appears that the Sgt. Clerk had told him he would have to go & he was therefore ~~unable~~ unaware that he could voluntarily defer his demobilization	
Oct.	19		Returns & Office Routine	
"	20		Met "Q" ~~at~~ and representatives of Units at Carlswerke Mülheim, at which factory their equipment was to be sent. Drew money from Field Cashier for men's pay. II Corps sent me back in a car – called at I.C.S. to arrange for some surplus stores to be sent there direct. Visited A. Battery H.A.C. 126 Bgde.	
"	21		Large quantities of Surplus Stores arrived from Units, which much handicapped me on account of	

D. D. & L., London, E.C. (A8004) Wt. W1771/M2031 750,000 5/17 Sch. 52 Forms/C2118/14

Instructions regarding War Diaries and Intelligence Summaries are contained in F. S. Regs., Part II. and the Staff Manual respectively. Title pages will be prepared in manuscript.

WAR DIARY
or
INTELLIGENCE SUMMARY.
(*Erase heading not required.*)

DDOS Southern Div.

Army Form C. 2118.

Place	Date	Hour	Summary of Events and Information	Remarks and references to Appendices
Odenthal	Oct 21		the small storage accommodation, and the necessity of transporting it by lorry to Railhead 5 miles distant. This is another proof of the unsuitability of Odenthal for an Ordnance Depot. Had Berg Gladbach be chosen instead, a great saving in petrol would have been made at least.	
			Visit from Adj. of 126 Bdge reference stores deficient to G1098	
			Sent representative to C.R.E. Burscheid to check & receipt for valuable stores.	
			Visited Div. Hqrs. "A" to ask for fatigue party of six men & one senior N.C.O. Visited Baths Officer, who again expressed his willingness to receive all the vests & drawers in bulk.	
			Obtained the use of a horse from 113 Brigade, which had been offered me by "Q".	
"	22		L/Cpl. Dedman went on leave. Valuable stores collected from Burscheid & Hermeskirchen. Large quantities of surplus stores still arrive. According to D.R.O. of Sept. 3 all surplus stores not required were to be handed into ordnance, and it seems that Units took advantage of the words "not required".	
			Rode to Burscheid & inspected Requisitioned stores of Field Coy.	

D. D. & L., London, E.C. (A8001) Wt. W1771/M2031 750,000 5/17 Sch. 52 Forms/C2118/14

Instructions regarding War Diaries and Intelligence Summaries are contained in F. S. Regs., Part II. and the Staff Manual respectively. Title pages will be prepared in manuscript.

WAR DIARY
or
INTELLIGENCE SUMMARY.
(*Erase heading not required.*)

DADOS Southern Div

Army Form C. 2118.

Place	Date	Hour	Summary of Events and Information	Remarks and references to Appendices
Odental	Oct 23		Visited Bdge Hqrs to obtain assistance of M.P to guard Surplus Dump. Reopened the question of Winter Underclothing being issued Direct from Baths with "Q" pointing out that G.R.O did not state that the first issue of cotton Drawers was to be made from Ordnance. "Q" agreed to the Drawers being all sent in Bulk to Baths Officer. This arrangement will greatly assist Ordnance and also the B.O. as he will be able to keep a Direct check on Units re returning their cotton Drawers.	
"	24		Visit from O.C. A Battery H.A.C. also from A.D.O.S. returned with him to Mulheim & visited 53rd Warwicks & I.C.S. Having no means of getting from Berg Gladbach to Odental, I remained there & billeted in A. Battery & H.A.C. quarters. Drew money from F.C.	
"	25		Returned to Odental on horseback. Office Routine	
"	26		Office Routine	
"	27		" & paid out.	
"	28		Visited all batteries of 113 Brigade to condemn a fairly large quantity of unserviceable harness. Bits were particularly	

D. D. & L., London, E.C.
(A8004) Wt. W1771/M2031 750,000 5/17 Sch. 52 Forms/C2118/14

Instructions regarding War Diaries and Intelligence Summaries are contained in F. S. Regs., Part II. and the Staff Manual respectively. Title pages will be prepared in manuscript.

WAR DIARY
or
INTELLIGENCE SUMMARY.
(Erase heading not required.)

DADOS
Southern Div

Army Form C. 2118.

Place	Date	Hour	Summary of Events and Information	Remarks and references to Appendices
	Oct.			
Odental	28		bad. One battery showed me 25 bits recently received to replace unserviceables, which were worse than those returned.	
			Called on C.R.A to ask for covering letter of harness condemned.	
"	29		Called on Div. Hqrs. to report that no list of Deficiencies or certificates that Surplus Stores had been handed in had been received from the Units. Called on C.R.A.	
			Received list of volunteers for R.A.O.C from D.O.S through A.D.O.S. with instructions to interview as many as possible & send the remainder to I.C.S. Southern Div "A" had already arranged to send me twelve men.	
"	30		Called on 1st Inf. Bde Hqrs re Volunteers for R.A.O.C to ask for certain men to be included in the twelve they were sending me. Visit from A.D.O.S. Drew blanket from Cologne. Visited 2nd Southern Inf. Bde.	
"	31.		Visited 1st " " " also Div. Hqrs to ask for 12 Volunteers for the R.A.O.C to be instructed to report to OO II Corps Troops. N.I.C.S. wrote asking for remainder of Volunteers to be sent to him. Units have again got into the bad habit of not making out their Indents in accordance	

B. D. & L., London, E.C. (A8004) Wt. W1771/M2031 750,000 5/17 Sch. 52 Forms/C2118/14

Instructions regarding War Diaries and Intelligence Summaries are contained in F. S. Regs., Part II. and the Staff Manual respectively. Title pages will be prepared in manuscript.

WAR DIARY
or
INTELLIGENCE SUMMARY.
(Erase heading not required.)

DDOS Southern Div

Army Form C. 2118.

Place	Date	Hour	Summary of Events and Information	Remarks and references to Appendices
Bristol	Oct 31		with instructions as per D.R.O. & G.R.O. (5521). Several sections are often on the same Indent, which is signed by an officer neither in command nor second in command. The Certificates are sometimes not struck out & if struck out are often not initialled. This only causes an unnecessary delay and it is entirely in the interest of the Units to make out their Indents properly. Informed "G" of this. A great amount of work & time would be saved if Units would follow carefully instructions laid down in D.R.O's & G.R.Os. If the Q.M.S in a battery is not competent to do this as regards Indents it would be a good plan if one of the Officers preferably the Capt. were to act as Quartermaster. Visited 52 Warwicks re volunteers for R.A.O.C. Was informed that 3 men had already been sent in. H.W. Elliott Lieut. R.G.A. a/DDOS Southern Div	

D. D. & L., London, E.C. (A8004) Wt. W1771/M2031 750,000 5/17 Sch. 52 Forms/C2118/14